AF553710

LITERACY
AND
DEVELOPMENT

LITERACY AND DEVELOPMENT

By

Dr. P. Adinarayana Reddy
Dept. of Adult and Continuing Education
Sri Venkateswara University
Tirupati–517 502 (A.P.)

DISCOVERY PUBLISHING HOUSE
NEW DELHI-110002

First Published-2005

ISBN 81-7141-942-9

Published by

DISCOVERY PUBLISHING HOUSE
4831/24, Ansari Road, Prahlad Street,
Darya Ganj, New Delhi-110002 (India)
Phone: 23279245 • Fax: 91-11-23253475
E-mail:dphtemp@indiatimes.com

Printed at:
Amit Enterprises, Delhi

Preface

The Government of India has formulated and implemented a number of adult education programmes to promote literacy among the masses to create opportunities and facilities to make use of it in their day-to-day life to improve their socio-economic status. But very few attempts have been made to assess the level of literacy retained and its impact on socio-economic development. Hence, the present study was an attempt in this direction.

The findings of the study were presented in seven chapters. The chapter I Introduction presents the background of the study and methodology adopted. The adult literacy programmes in Andhra Pradesh, literacy situation in the study area and sample of the study described in chapter II. The chapter III Retention of Literacy provides the extent of literacy retained by the neo-literates. The perception of neo-literates towards various programme factors was presented in the chapter IV. The chapter V presents the Impact of Literacy on Socio-economic Development of the neo-literates and Correlation among literacy, programme factors and socio-economic development in chapter VI. The Summary and Conclusions constituted the last chapter of the book.

The investigator expresses his gratitude to the University Grants Commission, New Delhi for providing financial assistance under the scheme of Major Research Projects for the present study. He also expresses his gratefulness to the entire sample for their co-operation in collection of data.

Dr. P. Adinarayana Reddy

Contents

1

Introduction

Recognising the relationship between level of literacy and economic development of the country, the Government of India has launched a number of educational programmes for the promotion of literacy among the adults in the age group of 15-35 years. However, the impact of these programmes in raising the literacy levels and socio-economic status of the people were found to be minimal due to lack of effective monitoring and follow-up. Realising the mistakes of the past and keeping in view the present day needs and demands the Government of India has established the National Literacy Mission (NLM). The aim of the NLM is to unversalise the literacy in the productive age group of 15-35 years and strengthen them by providing information relating to the national goals. As a result of this new strategy, all the districts in the country are being covered under Total Literacy Campaign in a phased manner.

Andhra Pradesh is recognised as one of the educationally backward states and the Total Literacy Campaign is being organised in all the districts. Andhra Pradesh is having three distinct geographical areas namely Rayalaseema, Telangana and coastal Andhra Pradesh. Among the three, Rayalaseema is considered to be backward both in terms of natural and human resources. Keeping in view of this, all the four districts in the region were given priority to launch the Total Literacy Campaign. All the four districts have already completed Total Literacy Campaign, post literacy programme and organising continuing education programme.

The success of any educational programme largely depends on the achievement of the objectives of the programme. In case of TLC, the success not only lies in literating the illiterates but also retaining them as literates and making them to utilise the newly learned skills of literacy in their day to day activities for their own betterment. In order to strengthen the programme, it is essential to evaluate the same to identify the strengths and weakness of the programme. This will help not only for strengthening the weak aspects of the programme but also to replicate the positive aspects.

The first phase of the programme i.e. literating the illiterates is over and the second phase of the programme i.e. retention and strengthening of the literacy is in operation through JANA CHAITYANYA KENDRAS and continuing education centres. In addition to the Kendra activities, the Zilla Shaksharatha Samithis are also distributing the fortnightly board sheet for promoting and strengthening the literacy. The literacy acquired during the literacy campaign is of fragile in nature and if not cultivated the new literates will be replacing into illiteracy. The investment of crores of rupees, time, men and materials invested on the programme will go a waste. Retention and strengthening of literacy will take some time and at the same time the impact of this strengthening and practising of the literacy will show a seed for a change.

The literacy acquired through the short-duration campaign approach is fragile in nature and if not properly nurtured there is every chance that the neo and semi-literates may surely relapsed into illiteracy. However if suitable environment was created to use the skill it is likely that the literacy will get strengthened and its usage in day-to-day spears of life will lead to improvement of the status of the individual in the society. Keeping in view of the above there is a need to study the extent of retention of literacy over a period of time so as to understand its effect on the individual with special reference to his status. Further it is also essential to understand the factors affecting the retention of literacy.

A review of research in this area was made to know the status of work that has been done, and to identify the gaps in this area. The available studies are review and presented in the following pages.

Status of Research

Research in the field of adult education is scanty, sporadic and still in its fancy. However, from the last decade the process of research in this field began establishing itself as one of the important social science discipline. A review of the research in this field indicates that majority of the studies are related to the evaluation of adult education programmes initiated at different periods of time. The survey reports of educational research (NCERT) has covered almost all the investigations undertaken in the field. Majority of the studies are Ph.Ds, dissertations and research projects, reports sponsored by various funding agencies. The available research can broadly be categorised into studies on NAEP, Total Literacy Campaigns and Post-literacy programmes.

The review of studies of NAEP, Total Literacy Programme and Post-Literacy Programmes are as follows. The review of the NAEP [Aikara (1984) and Acharji Mitra (1983), Mitra and Vanjoug (1983), Ganguli (1987), Ganguli Pathak and Misra (1983, 1984a, 1984b), Harihar and Rao (1982a, 1982b), Kantisen and Banerjee (1982), Leela Visaria (1984), Leela Visaria and Mathews (1983), Leela Visaria and Patel (1984), MIDS 1982a, 1982b, 1993, 1993a, 1985), Ramsankar (1982), Om Srivastava (1976), Pillai (1986, 1990) shows that these studies are aimed at assessing the literacy attainment, environment of the programme and looking into the personal background of the functionaries.

The studies on Total Literacy Campaigns (National Institute of Rural Development (1994), Council for Social Development (1993), Krishna Murthy and others (1982), University of Hyderabad (1992), Gopala Krishna Reddy (1994), Sardar Patel Institute of Economic and Social Research (1993) (1993a), (1993b), (1994), (1994a), Parekh (1991), Shantha Mohan (1991), Palu Vaikanadathial and Saravana (1994), Kishore Attavar (1993), Anil Bhatt (1993), Karve Institute of Social Sciences (1994), Deepak Kumar Behra (1992) (1992a), Tribal and Harizan Research cum Training Institute (1993), Mustaq Ahmed (1992) (1994), Tata Institute of Social Sciences (1993), Centre for Media Studies (1994), Zakir, Saravana Kumar and Meera Batra (1994), Indra Deva (1993), (1994), Om Mehta, Binore Deve and Sharma (1994), Mishra (1994), are aimed at measuring the literacy standards acquired by the participants.

The studies of the post-literacy programmes [Mustaq Ahmed (1958) (1957) (1985), Seth (1953), Asha (1972), IIALM (1997), Jansi Rani (1980), Sankar (1982), Srijayanthi (1982), Venkataiah and P.A. Reddy (1983).

Adinarayana Reddy (1985), Kalpana Mohanty (1987), Pati (1988) relates to the identification of reading interests, suitability of the materials, effectiveness of the functionaries and problems of the post-literacy workers etc.

In the area of retention of literacy, very few studies are carried out, most important among them are Pradipto Roy and Kapoor (1975), Mustaq Ahmed (1985) and Directorate of Adult Education (1991). Pradipto Roy and Kapoor (1975) identified the extent of retention of the literacy and socio-psychological factors contributing for the retention of literacy. Mustaq Ahmed (1985) identified the relationship between period of study and the extent of retention of literacy. The DAE (1991) also identified the extent of literacy retained by the ex-learners after a gap of 2 years.

The studies relating to the literacy and development are Harbison and Myers (1964) reported that among 75 nations, GNP per capita was correlated 67 with primary school enrolment, 82 with secondary school enrolment, and 0.74 with third level enrolment. Becker (1964) has made an analysis to show that men with more education make more money in their life time, even when ability and background variables are equated for those who go on to school as compared with those who do not. Becker's (1964) individual studies also suggest that more education preceded and made possible the increase in individual income. Shoup's (no date) study indicated that non-literate labour whether on land or in town earned considerably less than literate labour (Phillips, 1971, p. 35). "It has been shown that there is a significant correlations among countries between on the one hand the percentage of literacy and other hand per capita income industrialisation, political participation, and the reception of information media" (Golden, 1955). Bazany (no date, p. 127) found that achieved level in literacy by participants in work-oriented literacy courses in Iran did not contribute to the salary variation (r^2.61 per cent).

The Directorate of Adult Education (1972) found that the incomes of the participating farmers increased substantially. In Agra, the average income of functional literacy participants increased from Rs. 2,768 to 4,173, an increase of Rs. 1,405. The average income of non-participating farmers was Rs. 3,567. In Bangalore, the average income of the respondents from functional literacy group was about Rs. 1,471 as against an average of Rs. 1,000 in the control group. Also, the increase in income in the experimental group was reported to be to the tune of 100-200 per cent as against 50 per cent and less in the control villages.

UNESCO (Literacy 1969-71, pp. 30-31) reports that "when employed, the illiterate usually (but not always) earn lower wages than other workers. A study made by the Junta National de Plantification of Ecuador showed that 76.5 per cent illiterate workers earn less than 600 sucrase (U.S. @ 1 =

26 sucrase) monthly, while of workers with one to six years of primary schooling a much smaller 49.:3 per cent earn less than the figure. A study of the workers earnings in Brazil in 1963 shows that, "depending on the region in which they live, workers with basic literacy (primary-school level) earn on an average from 22 per cent to 35.5 per cent more than illiterate workers. According to a recent publication of the Board for Fundamental Education, a voluntary organisation in the United States, economists have estimated that 43 million Americans in the work force who have not finished high school could add as much as $ 100 billion to the GNP if they became more productive workers as a result of increased education" (UNESCO's Literacy, 1969-71, p. 29). Bastian and Ross (1962) found that the level of education and the level of income had little connection with differences at the farmers spent on mass media. Fliegel *et. al*. (1967, p. 55) found that the literacy was correlated strongly with per cent of families taxed Rs. 10 or more a year.

It is surprising to note that only very few attempts have been made to study the various aspects related to the retention of literacy, literacy and economic development. The knowledge in this area is essential in view of the faster expansion of the adult education programme and creation of large pool of the neo-literates. Further the aim of the present day adult education programme is not limited to adult literacy alone but also to accelerate the socio-economic scenario of the country. Hence, in view of the above, the present study is taken up to identify the extent of retention of literacy over a period of 3 years, factors contributing for the same, impact of literacy on socio-economic development as a whole. However, the specific objectives of the study are as follows:

Objectives of the Study

(i) To identify the level of retention of literacy among neo-literate over a period of 3 years.

(ii) To study the impact of programme factors on the of socio-economic development the neo-literates over a period of three years.

(iii) To study the influence of programme factors (environment, instruction and administration) and personal factors of neo-literates on the retention of literacy.

(iv) To study the nature of relationship between the retention and literacy and socio-economic and programme factors of neo-literates.

(v) To identify and study the influence of personal factors on socio-economic development and retention of literacy among neo-literates.

Hypothesis of the Study

In the light of the above objectives the following hypotheses were formulated for testing.

(i) The level of retention of literacy over a period of three years is not similar.

(ii) There exists no association between personal factors and retention of literacy.

(iii) There is no significant relation between personal factors and retention of literacy.

(iv) There is no significant influence of programmes factors on retention of literacy.

(v) There is no significant association between personal factors and socio-economic development.

(vi) There is no significant relationship between personal factors and socio-economic development.

(vii) There is no significant correlation between retention of literacy and socio-economic development.

Methodology

(i) *Local of the Study*

To study the level of retention of literacy among the neo-literates, the area and sample should be homogeneous in terms of geography, dialect of the language and socio-economic condition. Keeping in view of the above factors it was decided to choose the Rayalseema region of the Andhra Pradesh. This region consists of four districts. It is homogenous with background, uses same dialect with similar socio-economic conditions. Hence for the purpose of the present study Rayalseema region was selected as local of the study.

(ii) Sample of the Study

To study of level of retention of literacy and its impact on socio-economic development requires to choose suitable sample. Hence for the present study a stratified random sampling method was adopted for selecting the sample. In the first stage of sample selected ten mandals were selected randomly from each district. In the second stage from each mandal ten villages are selected randomly. In the last stage of sample selection, from each village five adult neo-literates were selected as sample of the present study. In addition to the above, from each district 25 field functionaries were selected to ascertain their views on the role of administrative aspects on retention of literacy. The sample frame of the study is as follows:

a.	No. of district	=	4
b.	No. of mandals	=	40
c.	No. of villages	=	400
d.	No. of learners	=	2000
e.	No. of field functionaries	=	100

The study covered 40 mandals, 400 villages, 2000 Neo-literates, 100 programme functionaries as sample of the study.

(iii) Data Gathering Devices

In order to test the hypothesis framed, certain information has to be collected from the selected sample. As the study aimed to identify the level of literacy retained over a period of three years and its impact on socio-economic development of the target, three devises viz., achievement test in literacy socio-economic development measure and a schedule to identify the programme factors are required. The review of literature revealed that there is no suitable and ready made research tools to measure the above. Hence, it was decided to develop the following tools.

(a) An achievement test in literacy covering the components of reading and writing and arithmetic.

(b) A schedule to measure the programme factors covering the aspects of environment, instructional and academic factors.

(c) A scale to measure the development of the neo-literates in terms of social development, economic development and socio-economic development due to literacy.

(a) Achievement Test in Literacy

For the purpose of the present study an achievement test in literacy was development. The measure of achievement in literacy is intended to estimate the level of attainment in reading, writing, arithmetic skills by the neo-literates. The programme participants who has successfully completed the course in Akshara Tapasman Programme should have achieved basic skills of reading, writing, Arithmetic to the extent of fulfilling the norms of literacy stipulated by National Literacy Mission.

Keeping in view of the above and based on the National Literacy Mission norms the investigator has developed 3 sub-tests in literacy viz Reading, Writing and Arithmetic.

I. Reading Test

The reading test is intended to identify the level of reading capabilities and proficiency retained by the neo-literates in reading. The items for the reading test were drawn from the primers utilised in the Akshara Tapasman Programme. The Reading test has 4 units namely (1) Reading of small passage (2) Reading of signs, (3) Understanding the messages and (4) Silent reading with understanding. The above items were considered for the test only after gathering the opinions of volunteers, monitors and experts in the field.

The primers that was used in Total Literacy Campaign was prepared based on the I.P.C.L. norm. In other words the participant will start learning not by alphabetic method but they start with simple sentences along with message. The evaluation in this primers are in built and there is no performance for alphabetic order but importance was accorded to the recognising the alphabets incorporated in the sentence. Further the experts and field functionaries advised the investigator not to include alphabets and simple words for achievement test as these are very preliminary as all the might have crossed this stage with in 3 months. Hence recognisation of the alphabets, simple words are not included in the test.

1. *Reading of Simple Para*

A simple passage consisting of 16 words ranging the words with 2 to 4 letters were given.

2. *Recognising the Signs*

A traffic sign showing the way to different places at a cross road with arrow marks drawn and presented. The intention of the test is whether the participants were able to understand the meaning attached to sign and whether they were able to read the names written on the arrow marks.

3. *Understanding the Massages Depicted on the Posters*

This test was designed to understand whether the participants were capable of understanding the massages depicted on the posters and advertisement panels. The poster as a mass media agency is being utilised widely for popularising the various messages. For example Anti-Arrack movement, population, consumer goods, pictures, development programmes etc. If the participants were capable of receiving the message of mass media in their development then the aim of the literacy is success. Keeping the above in view two posters on population explosion and Anti-Arrack movement were shown to the participants for their recognisation.

4. *Silent Reading with Understanding*

A passage consisting of 9 sentences, i.e., 33 words on Environment was prepared. The sample selected for the study is to supposed to read the passage silently with understanding and should be able to answer to the question orally. The intention of the test is whether they will be able to understand the message that was given in the passage. Hence the preliminary draft of the reading test was approached by drawing the content from the primers.

The preliminary form of the Reading Test thus finalised was administered to a sample of 100 neo-literates individually by the investigator. The data this obtained were analysed to find out the differences and discriminative level of the items incorporated in the preliminary form. As suggested by Garett (1979) all the items showing discrimination values of 0:30 and above and difficulty values between 0.40 and 0.60 as suggested by Liner Man were considered for inclusion in final form and rest of the items were ignored.

The final form of the Reading Test consisted of 4 units and scoring of the test were given as detailed below.

Table—1.1: Scoring procedure of reading test

Sl. No.	Items		Marks for each item
Unit	I	Reading of simple passage	7
Unit	II	Recognising of signs and reading of names of the places	3½
Unit	III	Massage recognition	3½
Unit	IV	Silent reading with comprehension	20
		Total	**34**

II. Development of Writing Sub Test

A review of the written test developed by different investigators shows that a comprehensive written test will have 6 sub-tests namely (1) Writing of alphabets (2) Writing of words (3) Writing of sentences (4) Writing of paragraph (5) Writing of letter/Application (6) Writing of answers to comprehensive questions based on the passage chosen for the purpose. However the experts and field functionaries consulted has suggested that it will be appropriate to include only 4 aspects namely (1) Copy writing, (2) Dictation, (3) Writing of memorandum, (4) Comprehensive reading and fill-in the banks. After finalising the format of the writing test the required items were generated from the primers used in the Akshara Tapasman Programme. Some of the items suggested by the experts and field functionaries were also incorporated in the test.

1. *Unit-I Copy Writing of Passage*

The passage consisting of 5 sentences, 20 words with letters ranging from 2 to 8 alphabets in a word was developed.

2. *Unit-II Dictation*

Under this unit, the respondents has to take down the words dictated by the investigator. Under this item, 8 words with 3 to 6 letters in each word was incorporated.

3. *Unit-III Writing a Memorandum/Letter Under*

This item the respondents were asked to write a memorandum representing the higher authorities about the common problems of the village or they can write a letter to their friends about the latest development in their village.

4. *Unit-IV Comprehension and fill-in the Blanks*

Under the item a passage consisting of 10 sentences with 60 words was given and the subjects were suppose to go through the passage and they have to fill the sentences that was given under the passage.

The preliminary form of written test was submitted to a panel of 5 subject experts for their comments, and suggestions. The suggestions of the experts were incorporated and revised the test. The revised test was administered to neo-literates individually. The data thus obtained was analysed to find out the difficulty and discrimination levels of each of the items representing the preliminary form. Item showing discrimination value of 0.30 and above and difficulty values between 0.40 and 0.60 were included in the final form.

The final form of writing test was represented by 4 units consisting of simple para of copy writing, taking down the dictation of 5 words, letter writing, completing 5 comprehensive sentences. The scoring procedure for the writing sub test in brief was as follows.

Table—1.2: Scoring procedure for writing test

Sl. No.		Item	Marks for each item
Unit	I	Copy writing (4 sentences 17 words)	3
Unit	II	Dictation	5
Unit	III	Memorandum/letter	20
Unit	IV	Filling up 5 in complete sentences	5
		Total	33

III. Development of Numeracy Sub Test

Before developing the numeracy test, all the available arithmetic tests developed in various projects were examined. The arithmetic test commonly contained additions, subtractions, multiplications, divisions and problems containing any one or combination of the above. In view of the above background, the investigator consulted the experts about the possible items to be incorporated in the test and experts suggestions were followed in developing the test.

The investigator pooled all the possible items to be incorporated in the test under different items, and these items were supplemented through the discussions with field staff and experts.

1. ***Unit-I Transfiguring***

Under this items 8 figures with 2 and 3 digits were given for transfiguring.

2. ***Unit-II Additions***

Arithmetic operation involving addition of 1, 2, 3 and 4 digit numbers in 2 and 3 rows of 4 items were given.

3. ***Unit-III Subtraction***

Arithmetic operation involving subtraction of 2, 3 and 4 digit numbers of 8 items were given.

4. ***Unit-IV Multiplication***

Arithmetic operations involving multiplication of 2, 3 and 4 digit numbers with sign and double digit numbers of 10 items were incorporated.

5. ***Unit-V Division***

Arithmetic operations involving division of 2, 3 and 4 digit number with single and double digit numbers of 8 items were given.

In addition to the above, under the unit-6 problems involving simple arithmetic operations namely addition, subtracting, multiplication. Division weights and measures, currency, time, distance were incorporated. Again the draft form of Arithmetic test was submitted to a panel of 5 experts and their suggestions was also incorporated by altering some of the problems.

The preliminary form thus prepared was administered to 100 neo-literates for tryout and for finalising the test. The data thus obtained was analysed to find out the difficulty and discrimination levels of each of the items representing the preliminary form. Items showing discrimination values ranging between 0.40 and 0.60 were considered for the final form. The final form of Arithmetic test consisted of 6 subunits. The details are as follows.

Table—1.3: Scoring procedure for arithmetic test

Sl. No.	Item	Sub-test	No. of item	Total marks
Unit	I	Transfiguring the numbers	4	2
Unit	II	Additions	4	i
Unit	III	Subtractions	4	4
Unit	IV	Multiplication	4	4
Unit	V	Division	4	4
Unit	VI	Problem		
	a	Simple problems	5	5
	b	Problem with combination of mathematics operations	5	10
		Total		**33**

6. *Reliability of the Test*

The reliability of the achievement test was established by adopting test re-test reliability of the 3 sub-tests were examined. This was done by administering the entire achievement test to the same set of 100 neo-literates with the gap of 3 weeks. The co-relation co-efficients between reading, writing, arithmetic sub tests was 0.93, 0.91, 0.89 respectively. The 'r' values of the sub tests were significant at 0.01 level. In view of this, test can be considered having high reliability.

7. *Validity of the Test*

The test developed for measuring a particular aspect will be considered appropriate only when its validity is true. The achievement test in 3R's developed on the lines described above possess satisfactory validity with reference to the content and intrinsic validity.

8. *Achievement Test in Brief*

The test consisted of 3 sub-tests namely reading test, writing test and arithmetic test etc. The reading sub test consisted of reading of simple passage, recognisation of signs, understanding the posters and message incorporated and silent reading with comprehension. The writing sub-test included copy writing, dictation, writing of memorandum/ application, comprehension and filling the in-complete sentences. The Arithmetic sub-test includes transfiguring, additions, subtractions, multiplications, division, simple problems and problems involving combination of different arithmetic operation.

Thus maximum possible scores for reading is 40 and 30 each for writing and arithmetic. Thus for the achievement test the total maximum possible score is 100 marks. The test require about, 50-60 minutes to complete it. The reading sub-test can be administered only individually where as the writing and arithmetic sub tests can be administered to a small groups.

(b) Schedule to Identify the Programme Factors

Success of any educational programme lies in achieving the objectives for which it was formulated. In case of Adult literacy programme the success of the programme lies in promoting the literacy. The promotion of literacy among the illiterates also depends on no. of factors, among them the programme factors constitutes one of the important factor. The programme factors includes the environment where the programme was organised, the instructional aspects and administrative aspects in view of the above a thorough review of literature was made to locate the tools used to identify the above. The search revealed that very few attempts were made and they are not relevant to present contexts. Hence it was decided to develop a schedule to measure the programme aspects so as to related it to the retention of literacy.

The items related to the programme aspects mainly the environment of the centre, location, physical facilities available, proximity, regularity in attendance co-operation and encouragement given by the family members, peer group, community members, participation of friends and other family members constitute the environmental factors. The instructional aspects of the programme relates to the teaching, learning materials, relevance and usefulness of the content, availability of the materials, methods of teaching, time spent by the learners in the centre etc.

The administrative aspects of the programme include the performance of volunteer in terms of public relations, teaching, attention to the learners, creation of infrastructural facilities discipline etc. suitability of volunteer interms of age, sex, caste as viewed by the learners etc., keeping the above aspects in view a list of items reflecting the administrative factors were prepared and presented to a panel of five experts with a request to go through the items delete the redundant and duplicated items and to add missing items. The suggestions of the experts were incorporated. A provision was created for all the items to provide responses by the sample. The schedule thus prepared was administered to a sample of 50 neo-literates to study its workability and usefulness. Based on the response pattern a few items were modified and finalised the schedule. The final format of the schedule was enclosed in the annexure.

(c) Constriction of a Socio-economic Development Measure

Keeping in view of the above available evidences for the impact of literacy on socio and economic development of an individual, it was decided to study the changes that will be visible due to acquisition of literacy in the social spear of life. The review of the studies relating to social development due to possession of literacy-shows that changes will occur in the areas of social participation, communication with the other, membership in socio-cultural organisations, improved contacts with the official, community leaders, political leaders, use of institutions, exposure to different media and using those media for self development, adoption of new methods, change in occupation, possession and modernisation of occupational instruments and household articles, understanding the problems causes and consequences, ability to formulate suitable strategy to overcome them etc. Further it was also revealed that there is no comprehensive single tool to measure the social development of an individual.

Keeping in view of the above it was decided to develop a tool to measure the social development of individual. Further it should have a provision to reveal the extent of improvement in social development. As a first step in this direction the investigator has collected the items depicting the social status of an individual in the society. These items are collected by interacting with the sociologists, educators, adult education functionaries etc. The items thus pooled are from the different spears of social life. The items thus collected were supplemented with the list of items drawn from review of literature. The list at this stage consisted of 35 items. The list of items were presented to a panel of experts for their scrutiny and suggestions to delete the retardant and ambiguous and items which are not depicting the social status and also to suggest additional items if required. The suggestions were incorporated. The final list of items thus prepared was administered to a sample of 50 neo-literates to study its workability and response pattern of the sample. Based on the response pattern, the items were classified under different headings and some were deleted. Further a provision was created to provide response either in the form of acceptance and in some cases a five point scale to provide responses. The final format of the social development scale was presented in the Appendix.

The economic status of an individual is reflected through the possession of household articles and the income earned by the individual through different means. The available economic development scales are not broad based taking in to the consideration of the characteristics and background of the sample of the present study. Hence the investigator decided to develop a simple instrument capable of measuring the economic status of an individual. The scale was devised in such way that even if there is small charge in the economic spear it will reflect the same.

The items incorporated in the scale reflects the income of the family type of house facilities in the house, possession of land, jewellry, cattle, household, modern gadgets such as cycle, motor-cycle, Radio, T.V. furniture, wall clock, swing machine type of vessels, modern agricultural equipments etc. The scale thus developed as a provision to respond by the sample about the possession of the item or not. The scale thus developed was administered to a sample of 50 neo-literates to find out its segregating capacity based on their income. The analysis of the data shows that the scale is capable of performing the task for which it was devised.

(a) Scoring of the Items

In order to identify the level of social development it was decided to give a quantified score for all the items i.e. for the membership in self help group one mark was assigned. If some body is in more than one group then additional mark for every group way given in case of relationship with Government officials and political leaders and performance of tasks connected with literacy a five point scale with five cues i.e. very high, high, neutral, low, and very low was given. The sample is expected to go through the items and extent of the performance of the task should be checked in one of the given five alternatives. The sum of score constitute the status of the individual in social development.

In case of economic development the possession of household articles and others a mark was assigned to each item. For housing, a *pakka* house was given-3, marks shed-2, hut-1 marks and if more than one room, one mark was assigned for every additional room. Further more than 150 sq. feet for every additional sq. feet one mark was assigned, one mark each for bathroom and latrine was also given. In case of landed property less than 1 mark and for every additional acre additional mark was assigned. In case of cattles one mark was assigned for every cattle. One mark for jewellry worth of 1000 was given. The sum of all the above reflects the economic status of the neo-literates. The above criteria was used to measure the social development, economic development and socio-economic development by pooling the scores of the above.

Data Collection

The tools thus developed was administered to the selected sample. The achievement test and socio-economic development scale was administered to all the selected sample of neo-literate exactly after one year of the internal evaluation of the programme and later second and third year. The test was administered the same sample. Where ever the sample is not available for second and third administration, sample was substituted with similar. However care was taken not to cross 5% of the substitute sample. As a result, the investigator was forced to spend a lot of time and energy to relocate the same sample. The schedule relating to the programme aspects was also administered to the sample, along with the achievement test of the literacy. However the schedule to measure the programme aspects was administered only once and the same scores were utilised to study its effect retention of literacy. Before administering the above tools a good rapport was established with the sample and explained to them about the study and ways and means of filling the tools. The sample co-operated with the investigator and readily filled the tools.

Analysis of the Data

The informations thus collected from the sample was polled together and analysed the data keeping in view of the objectives of the study. The statistical techniques like 't' test, 'F' test 'chi' test was used to draw the inference. The chi test was applied to study the association between personal factors and retention of literacy. The 'F' test and 't' test was used to find out the differences if any among the different groups of sample in their retention of literacy and socio-economic development. The simple correlation was applied to study the co-relation between the social economic development and extent of retention of literacy among the neo-literates.

2

Adult Literacy Programme in Andhra Pradesh

Profile of the Study Area and the Sample

Andhra Pradesh is one of the educationally backward states with three distinct geographical regions viz. Rayalaseema, Telangana and Coastal Andhra. The state has 23 districts. The Rayalseema consists of 4 districts, Telangana with 10 Districts and Coastal has nine districts. As per 2001 census, it has a population of 75,727,541. Out of this 55,223,944 are from rural area and rest 20,503,597 are from urban area. In terms of sex, male (38,286,811) has an edge over female (37,440,730). Same trend prevails in the rural and urban areas.

Status of Literacy in Andhra Pradesh

As per 2001 census, the literacy rate of Andhra Pradesh is 6.11 per cent. Male and Female literacy rates are 70.85 and 51.17 per cent respectively. Rural and Urban literacy rate is 55.33 per cent and 76.33 per cent respectively.

During the decade 1991-2000, literacy rate of the state has increased by 17.02 per cent from 44.09 per cent to 61.11 per cent. During the same period, it is reported that the female literacy rate has increased by 18.4 per cent i.e., from 32.72 per cent to 51.17 per cent and the male literacy rate by 15.72 per cent from 55.13 per cent to 70.85 per cent. In literacy rate Andhra Pradesh is ranked 27th according to census 2001, and it was ranked 28th according to 1991 census.

Status of Total Literacy Campaigns in Andhra Pradesh

All the 23 districts in the state have taken up total literacy campaign. The target of the TLC's is 144.29 lakhs and learners enrolled is 128.44 lakhs. Out of them 80.451 lakhs have completed the primer III. All the districts have been evaluated both internally and externally.

According to the external evaluation of the total literacy campaign in the state range between 9.24 per cent in Prakasam District to 92.70 per cent in Visakhapatnam. The details of the percentage of literacy achieved by the districts as per external evaluation are Srikakulum (82.05%), Vizianagaram (39.10%), Visakhapatnam (92.70%) East Godavari (30.9%), West Godavari (81.79%), Krishna (41.74%), Guntur (46%) Prakasam (6.4%), Nellore (57.08%), Chittor (64.75% and 81.60%), Cuddapah (60%) Anantapur (37.80%), Kurnool (20%), Mahabubnagar (32%), Rangareddy (49%), Hyderabad (68.97%), Medak (32.54%), Nizamabad (63.19%), Karimnagar (92.3%), Warangal (13%), Khammam (33%) and Nalgonda (43%).

Post Literacy Programme in Andhra Pradesh

The post literacy programme was launched in all the districts with a target of 75.68 lakhs. However, the enrolment is only' 62.05 lakhs. The achievement of the neo-literates in terms of completion of the PL-I primer is only 44.26 lakhs. Under Post Literacy Programme Rs. 3434.51 lakhs was released. Out of it NLM has released 1,96,36,62 lakhs and State Government has released 1,497,89 lakhs. Out of this, 3097.68 lakhs was the expenditure. There is a large time gap between the closure of the TLC and launching of the Post-literacy Programmes. Though the programme was implemented by all the districts, no district was evaluated externally to study its impact.

Continuing Education Programme

All the districts in the state have completed Total Literacy Campaign and Post Literacy Programme. For the benefit of the neo-literates, the scheme of continuing Education was sanctioned to 20 districts of Andhra Pradesh. They are Srikakulam, Visakhapatnam, West Godavari, Nellore, Chittoor, Cuddapah, Nizamabad, Karim Nagar, Vizianagaram, Krishna, Ranga Reddy, Hyderabad, Medak, Warangal, Khammam, Anantapur, Guntur, Nalgonda and Prakasam.

It is reported that 2,189 Nodal Continuing Education Centres and 16,531 Continuing Education Centres have been sanctioned to these districts. Out of which, 1,568 NCECs and 13,079 CECs have been established. In all, 52.24 lakh persons have been taken advantage of these centres. for maintaining the above centres, NLM has released 2,144.56 lakhs as its share.

Akshara Sankranthi Programme

The Government of Andhra Pradesh is implementing Akshara Sankranthi Programme (ASP) for the benefit of left overs, drop outs, new entrants. The first phase of the Programme was started in 2000-2001, second phase in 2001-2002 and 3rd phase in 2002-2003 and fourth phase of the programme (2003-2004) was already launched.

The enrollment and achievement of the ASP of the 1st phase is 53.23 lakhs and 28.36 lakhs respectively. In case of 2nd phase, the enrollment is 38.23 lakhs and achievement is 22.75 lakhs.

Literacy Situation in Rayalaseema Region

The region wise literacy in Andhra Pradesh from 1971 to 2001 shows that the growth of literacy was not uniform. The coastal districts have attained a maximum literacy of 62.56 per cent in three decades and the Rayalaseema (60.65) and Telengana (58.08) followed the soute. Within the districts of Rayalaseema region, Chittoor has attained better position in literacy (67.46) when compared with the other districts in same period. After Chittoor, Cuddapah district has attained (64.02%) followed by Ananthapur (56.69) and Kurnool (54.43%).

The Rayalaseema region consisting of the districts of Chittoor, Cuddapah, Ananthapur and Kurnool. It occupies 27.4 per cent of the area of the states. The region is known for famine, sparsely populated and economically backward part of state. The soil is rocky and unyielding, the rainfall is scanty and uncertain. Agriculture is the main occupation of the area.

Table—2.1: Population, literates and illiterates in Rayalaseema region from 1951 to 2001

Sl. No.	Census Year	Total Population (in lakhs only)	No. of illiterates (in lakhs only)	No. of Literates	% of Literacy
1.	1951	56.56	48.54	8.02	14.18
2.	1961	69.54	54.67	14.66	21.14
3.	1971	79.41	80.18	19.42	24.40
4.	1981	96.25	67.22	29.04	30.17
5.	1991	116.85	72.94	43.29	44.96
6.	2001	116.99	46.17	70.81	60.65

The sex wise literacy rates in the region shows that again Chittoor (14.4%) literacy rate among women in 1971 roles to 56.28 whereas in case of Kurnool only 12.7% in 1971 and roses to 47.71. When compared with Cuddapah and Ananthapur, Cuddapah has attained 56.76 per cent among women where as Ananthapur could not cross 43.87 per cent.

Table—2.2: Region wise growth of literacy in Andhra Pradesh and Rayalaseema districts

S. No.	Region/District	Period			
		1971	1981	1991	2001
Andhra Pradesh					
1.	Coastal	27.7	32.8	46.9	62.56
2.	Rayalaseema	24.4	29.9	46.4	60.65
3.	Teleangana	20.7	26.6	41.4	58.08
Rayalaseema					
1.	Chittoor	25.04	31.4	51.8	67.46
2.	Cuddapah	24.7	31.1	50.2	64.02
3.	Kurnool	23.6	26.9	40.7	54.43
4.	Ananthapur	23.8	28.5	42.9	56.69

The area wise literacy variations of the districts in 2001 shows that again it is Chittoor which has 63.67 per cent in rural areas where as it is 80.94 in urban areas. In case of Cuddaph it is 61.14 per cent in rural areas and 73.41 per cent in urban areas. In case of Ananthapur the urban literacy rate is 70.23 per cent followed by 52.04 per cent in rural areas. However in case of Kurnool it is found to be 50.83 in rural and 66.48 in urban areas.

Table—2.3: Literacy rates among men and women in Rayalaseema region

Sl. No.	District	1971		1981		1991		2001	
		Men	Women	Men	Women	Men	Women	Men	Women
1.	Chittoor	35.9	14.4	42.7	19.8	65.1	38.2	78.29	56.48
2.	Cuddapah	36.2	12.7	43.8	17.7	65.8	33.9	76.98	50.76
3.	Ananthapur	34.7	12.4	40.2	16.5	56.9	28.3	68.94	43.87
4.	Kurnool	34.5	12.7	39.6	17.0	53.9	26.9	67.36	41.07

The area wise and sex wise literacy rates shows that Chittoor district rural women has attained 51.85 per cent of literacy whereas Kurnool has attained only 36.5 per cent among women, where as in case of urban areas again Chittoor has attained 73.04 per cent and Kurnool has attained 56.41 per cent among urban areas. In case of men Chittoor has reached 88.62 per cent where as Kurnool has attained 76.22 per cent in urban male population. The Kadapa and Anantapur has attained in between Chittoor and Kurnool in both rural and urban areas.

Table—2.4: Literacy rates among rural and urban areas in Rayalaseema region

Sl. No.	District	Rural		Urban		Rural	Urban
		Men	Women	Men	Women		
1.	Chittoor	73.56	51.85	88.26	73.04	63.67	80.94
2.	Cuddapah	75.02	46.94	83.43	63.21	61.14	73.41
3.	Ananthapur	65.13	38.13	80.10	59.99	52.04	70.23
4.	Kurnool	64.72	36.50	76.22	56.41	50.83	66.48

From the above it is clear that there is a wide variations of literacy rates in the area among different sex groups and area wise and district wise. In order to bridge the gaps between the extremes conserted effects are been made to promote literacy in these districts by launching total literacy campaigns, post literacy programme and continuing education programmes. As a result of these effects the literacy percentage was increased considerably by the end of 2001. However in view of the above observations it is not only necessary to consolidate the games but also to improve the literacy percentage, to reduce the literacy variations among the extreme groups.

Characteristics of the Sample

For the purpose of the present study, 2000 neo-literates were drawn from all over the four districts of Rayalaseema Region of Andhra Pradesh. In order to study the characteristics of the sample, the sample were classified into different groups based on their socio-economic and demographic characteristics. The classification of the sample enable to understand the proportional representation of various groups of participants in the programme. The details of the sample are presented in the following table.

(i) Sex Composition of the Sample

The sample selected for the study consists of both men and women neo-literates of the programme. Out of the sample, 60 per cent of them are women and 40 per cent are men. The trend of the sample is a true picture of the participation of the both the sex groups in the Adult Literacy Programme. Further, it is true that majority of the participants of the Adult Literacy Programmes are women as they were motivated to participate in the programme by using different strategies to improve the literacy rate among women.

(ii) Age Composition of the Sample

The age-wise division of the sample revealed that majority of the neo-literates selected for the study are from 30 and above years of age i.e., elders. The neo-literates in the age group of less than 20 years of age formed the third group. The picture clearly reveals that the participation of the adults in the age group of less than 20 years is less as majority of the people in this group are literates are very few of them were found to be target of Adult Education due to their discontinuation of their studies in their early period of schooling. Contrary to the above, majority of the target for the programme are found to be elders with more than 30 years of the age. The trend of the selected sample of the neo-literates are found to be a true representation of the universe of the study.

Table—2.5: Characteristics of the sample

Sl. No.	Character	Group	N	Per cent
1.	Sex	Men	8.00	40.00
		Women	12.00	60.00
2.	Age	Young	500	25.00
		Middle	700	35.00
		Elders	800	40.00
3.	Caste	OC	500	25.00
		BC	800	40.00
		SC/ST	700	35.00
4.	Exposure to Education	3 years	580	29.00
		2 years	380	19.00
		1 year	1040	52.00
5.	Occupation	Labour	540	27.00
		Agriculture	1180	59.00
		House wives	380	14.00
6.	Income	Low	740	32.00
		Middle	940	47.00
		High	420	21.00
7.	Type of family	Joint	760	38.00
		Nuclear	1240	62.00
8.	Marital status	Married	1200	60.00
		Unmarried	800	40.00
9.	No. of children	No child	980	49.00
		1 child	420	21.00
		2 >	600	30.00

(iii) Caste Composition of the Sample

In order to understand the representation of different caste group in the study, the sample were classified into 3 groups as forward castes, backward castes and SC/STs. The representation of the sample from different caste groups discloses that majority of them (40%) are from backward castes followed by with equal representation (25% each) from forward castes and scheduled castes/scheduled tribes. The proportion of representation clearly represents the size of their population in the total population of the sample area.

(iv) Earlier Exposure to Education

In order to study the earlier exposure of the sample to the education, the sample were classified into three groups with one year of exposure, two years of exposure and 3 and 4 years of exposure. The classification presented in the tables discloses that 52 per cent of the sample have exposed to the education/ adult education only for one year. It clearly shows that half of the samples selected for the study are illiterates without prior exposure to the education. Whereas 29 per cent of them revealed that they have exposed earlier to the education for 3 to 4 years indicating that they were either dropouts of formal system of education or earlier Adult Literacy Programme. In addition to the above 19 per cent of them also revealed that they have also exposed to education for 2 years. The overall trend of the exposure to the education makes clear that majority of the neo-literates selected for the study are the products of Adult Literacy Programmes.

(v) Occupation of the Sample

Occupation-wise distribution of the sample presented in the table shows that majority of them are from agricultural background followed by labourers (27%), and house wives (14%). The trend clearly shows that majority of them are from lower economic status depends on agriculture for their livelihood and also, found to be from rural areas. All the districts from the Rayalaseema Region depends on agriculture for their livelihood. The representation of the sample is found to be similar to the characteristics of the universe of the study.

(vi) Income Levels of the Sample

The selected sample were classified into 3 groups as low, middle and high income groups based on their income levels. The sample with less than Rs. 6,000/- per annum income were considered as middle income groups and those who have Rs. 12,000/- per annum and more income were considered as high income group. The above classification yielded 47 per cent of the sample as middle income group followed by 32 per cent as low income group and 21 per cent as high income group. The trend reveals that more than three fourths of them are from below poverty line group and 21 per cent belongs to above poverty line.

(vii) Type of Family

Based on the family background, the sample were classified into 2 groups as neo-literates from joint family and nuclear families. The division of the sample based on the above criteria revealed that 62 per cent of them have represented from nuclear families and 38 per cent of them are from joint families. This clearly indicates that the majority of the sample are from nuclear families, indicating that they have separated from their original families recently.

(viii) Marital Status of the Sample

Out of the 2000 samples of the study, 1,200 of them are found to be married and 800 are unmarried. In other words, 60 per cent of the selected sample are from married groups and the rest of them are from unmarried groups.

(ix) Number of Children

The sample also classified into 3 groups as no child group, one child group and 2 and above children groups. The classification revealed that about half of the sample does not have children. (This groups also consists of unmarried persons). Further 30 per cent of them have 2 and more children and 21 per cent of them are having one child. This clearly shows that majority of the sample are young and not burdened with the children. This discloses the less interference of the family affairs in learning.

Sum-up

The profile of the selected sample of the study discloses that majority of them are women, elders, backward castes, literates of Adult Literacy Programmes, Agriculturists, middle income groups, nuclear families, married and no children groups. This shows the profile of the Adult Education participants. However, the profile also shows that men, young, forward caste and SC/STs, 2 years of exposure to education, housewives, more income group, joint families, unmarried, one child groups of adults are found to be less participating in Adult Education Programmes. Hence, efforts should be made to increase their participation to acquire the literacy and utilise it for their socio-economic development.

3

Retention of Literacy

The success of Adult Literacy Programme lies in literating illiterates, retaining the literacy for a longer period and creating opportunities and environment for the neo-literates to utilise the newly learnt skills to improve their socio-economic conditions. No doubt, to make such a programme a success, a number of factors both internal and external to the programme will contribute.

Keeping in view of the above, an attempt was made to study the extent of retention literacy over a period of 3 years. Further, the factors contributed or otherwise for retaining the literacy were also identified.

Retention of Literacy Among the Neo-Literates

In order to identify the level of literacy attained and retained by the neo literates over a period of 3 years, the literacy achievement test designed for the purpose of the study was administered to the same set of the sample thrice at an interval of one year. Wherever the sample is missing, alternative sample with similar background and status were substituted. The collected data were pooled analysed and presented in the following table.

The results presented in the table shows that the attainment of the sample in reading was 32.98 during the first year. It was 33.37 at the end of second year and stabilised at 32.26 at the end of the third year. The trend of the mean achievement scores in reading clearly shows that the retention in reading has slightly increased in the second year and it has decreased in the third year. Further, the calculated 'F' value was found to be lower than the table value indicating that there is no significant changes in the mean retention scores in reading over a period of three years. The mean achievement scores obtained by the sample in writing presented in the table reveals that it is 21.50 during the first year, 20.73 in the second year and 20.33 at the end of the third year. The trend clearly shows that there is a loss of writing skills over a period of three years. However, the calculated 'F' value shows that the loss of skills is not significant. It indicates that the loss of skills is marginal.

Table—3.1: Mean retention scores, SD's obtained by the sample over a period of 3 years in reading, writing, arithmetic and literacy along with 'F' values

Sl. No.	Year	Reading			Writing			Arithmetic			Literacy		
		Mean	SD	'F' value	Mean	SD	'F' value	Mean	SD	'F' value	Mean	SD	'F' value
1.	First year	32.98	4.22		26.00	4.12		21.31	4.03		75.21	10.19	
2.	Second year	33.37	3.49	1.82@	20.73	3.92	0.68@	20.44	3.16	1.29@	74.65	8.62	0.62@
3.	Third	32.26	4.64		20.33	4.17		21.10	4.26		73.70	10.18	

@ Not significant

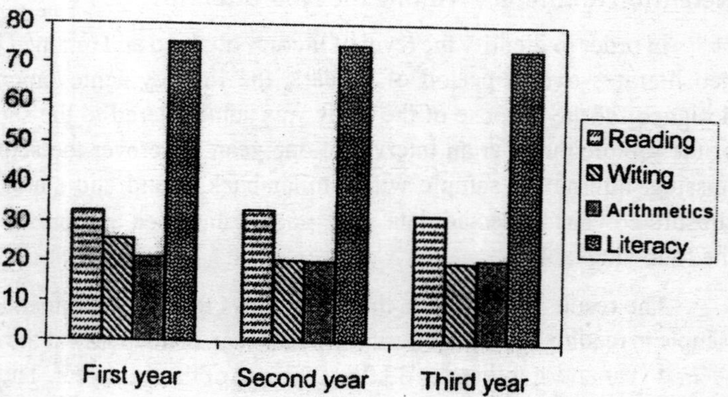

Fig. 1: Retention of Literacy over a period of 3 years

The trend of the mean achievement scores in numeracy by the sample revealed that it is 21.31 mean score at the end of the first year. At the end of the second year it is 20.44 and 21.10 at the end of the third year. The trend shows that there is an overall loss of mean arithmetic retention over a period of the three years. However, the calculated 'F' value revealed that it is not significant indicating that the mean attainment scores in numeracy are not significantly different from each other.

The attainment of the sample in literacy as a whole was found to be 75.21, 74.65 and 73.70 at the end of the first, second and third years respectively. The trend also reveals that there was a gradual loss of literacy skills over a period of three years. However, the calculated 'F' value revealed that the loss of skill is not significant.

The trend of the mean retention scores in reading, writing, arithmetic and in total literacy were found to be neither constant nor increased but gradually decreased. However the calculated 'F' values between first, second and third year for different components was found to be not significant. Hence the hypothesis "the level of retention of literacy over a period of three years is not similar" is accepted as there is no significant variation. This clearly shows that the literacy skills attained by the neo-literates during the programme period could not be strengthened significantly. In other words, the neo-literates have not used the skills in their day-to-day life to improve their skills. Further, it appears that they does not have suitable environment, opportunities to use the newly learned skill. It clearly demonstrates that the Post-Literacy and Continuing Education Programme conceived and implemented for strengthening and promotion of literacy were found to be not beneficial to the neo-literates either in strengthening the skills or in promotion of the skills. However, the existing environment hardly helped the neo-literates to gain the skills that they have attained due to their participation in Adult Literacy Programmes.

Keeping in view of the above pattern, the programme planners and administrators should take adequate measures to re-structure the Post Literacy and Continuing Education Programmes to create educative environment to practice and use the literacy skills by the neo-literates in their day-to-day life. The process should also help the neo-literates to strengthen the skills already learned and go for further education.

The Post Literacy and Continuing Education Programme should create enthusiasm and new learning needs among the neo-literates so as to enable them to utilise the existing skills and demand for advanced information for their furtherance.

Association Between Personal Characteristics and Retention of Reading Skill

The retention of any skill learnt not only depends on its regular usage but also depends on the personal background of the person who has acquired it. Keeping in view of the above, an attempt was made in the following pages to study the nature of association between the personal characteristics and extent of retention of reading skill over a period of 3 years. As a first step in this direction, the neo-literates are classified into different groups based on their personal characteristics calculated their respective mean reading retention skill and applied in the chi-test. Based on the above analysis the obtained results are presented in the Table—3.2.

Table—3.2: The chi-values obtained between the personal characteristics and retention of reading at the end of first, second and third year

Sl. No.	Personal Character	Ist Year	IInd Year	IIIrd Year
1.	Sex	2.21@	10.38*	5.73@
2.	Age	4.47@	2.58@	2.70@
3.	Caste	7.00@	4.472@	5.68@
4.	Exposure to Education	8.40@	3.68@	0.72@
5.	Occupation	2.78@	6.41@	0.87@
6.	Income	1.19@	17.05**	7.76@
7.	Type of Family	6.76*	1.16@	0.22@
8.	Marital Status	1.38@	2.22@	2.47@
9.	No. of Children	3.05@	10.15**	1.46@

The results relating to the association between the mean reading retention and personal characteristics shows that at the end of first year it was found that the association is not significant except in case of type of family. The results revealed that the role of personal characteristics are found to be not significant in retention of reading skills by the neo-literates. However it was found that there is a significant association between type of the family of the neo-literates and the retention of reading skill among the neo-literates at the end of first year.

At the end of the second year the results shows that the role of personal variables viz., sex, income and no. of children of the neo-literates has a significant role in retention of literacy among the neo-literates. However it was also revealed that the age, caste, exposure to formal education, occupation, type of family and marital status does not have a role in the retention of literacy among the neo-literates. The trend of the association between personal variables and the retention of the reading skill among the neo-literates at the end of 3rd year was found to be not significant. This shows that the role of personal variables on retention of reading skills was found to be not significant. Hence these need not be given prominence while promoting retention of reading skills. The association between personal variables and retention of reading skills over a period of 3 years shows that the association is not significant except in case of type of family at the end of first year, and sex, income and no. of children at the end of second year.

Association Between Personal Characteristics and Retention of Writing Skills

It was assumed that the retention of writing skills are not only based on the practical usage and practice of working skill but also based on the personal characteristics. In order to test the above assumption, the neo-literates are classified into different groups based on their personal characteristics and their respective mean writing skills was pooled at the end of first year, second year and third year and applied the chi-test. The findings of the above analysis are presented in the table.

Table—3.3: The chi-values obtained between the personal characteristics and retention of writing at the end of first, second and third year

Sl. No.	Personal Character	Ist Year	IInd Year	IIIrd Year
1.	Sex	5.77@	0.17@	7.20*
2.	Age	11.55**	4.29@	8.03@
3.	Caste	2.76@	4.03@	11.55*

(Table Contd...)

4.	Exposure to Education	10.75*	0.40@	1.44@
5.	Occupation	2.18@	2.37@	4.84@
6.	Income	15.49**	4.39@	8.57@
7.	Type of Family	0.39@	0.17@	0.44@
8.	Marital Status	2.82@	1.65@	1.46@
9.	No. of Children	3.97@	5.23@	9.90*

@ Not significant

* Significant at 0.05 level

** Significant at 0.01 level

The results presented in the table clearly reveals that the association between the sex, caste, and no. of children are found to be closely associated with the retention of writing skills among the neo-literates over a period of 3 years. However association between other personal characteristics viz., age, earlier exposure to education, occupation, income, type of family and marital status are found to be not significant indicating that their role is minimal in retention of writing skills.

The findings at the end of second year discloses that there is no significant association between the personal characteristics and the retention of writing skills at the end of second year indicating that personal characteristics has no role in retention of writing skills. However the obtained chi-values at the end of first year revealed that the role of age, earlier exposure of education and income of the neo-literate was found to be significant in retention of writing skill. Further it also reveals that insignificant role of sex, caste, occupation, type of family, marital status and number of children in retention of writing skills.

On the whole it appears that the age, earlier exposure to education, income (at the end of first year) sex, caste and number of children has played a significant role in retention of writing skills among the neo-literates over a period of 3 years.

Association Between the Personal Characteristics and Retention of Arithmetic Skill

In order to find out the association between the personal characteristics and retention of writing skills among the neo-literates, the neo-literates are classified into different groups based on their personal characteristic, calculated their respective mean Arithmetic scores and applied chi-test. The calculated chi-values between personal characteristics and retention of writing skills are presented in the table.

Table—3.4: The chi-value obtained between the personal characteristics and retention of arithmetic at the end of first, second and third year

Sl. No.	Personal Character	Ist Year	IInd Year	IIIrd Year
1.	Sex	0.96@	3.74@	1.22@
2.	Age	3.21@	12.93*	5.25@
3.	Caste	2.07@	0.79@	5.35@
4.	Exposure to Education	6.22@	1.85@	6.49@
5.	Occupation	10.15*	1.83@	6.18@
6.	Income	4.61@	3.59@	9.21@
7.	Type of Family	1.91@	1.21@	1.45@
8.	Marital Status	0.67@	0.51@	9.25@
9.	No. of Children	6.53@	0.63@	3.28@

@ Not significant
* Significant at 0.05 level
** Significant at 0.01 level

The results relating to the association between the retention of arithmetic skills and personal characteristics shows that the role of personal characteristics on retention of arithmetic skills are found to be non significant except in case of occupation at the end of first year and age at the end of second year. In other words the personal characteristics of the neo-literates has no role in retention of arithmetic skills among the neo-literates. Hence these need not be given prominence while organising post-literacy and continuing education programmes.

Association Between Personal Characteristics and Retention of Literacy

In order to study the association between personal characteristics and retention of literacy among the neo-literates the neo-literates were classified into different groups based on their personal characteristics calculated their respective mean literacy retention scores and applied chi-test to study the significant association if any. The obtained results of the chi-test was presented in the table 3.5.

Table—3.5: The chi-values obtained between the personal characteristics and retention of literacy at the end of first, second and the third year

Sl. No.	Personal Character	Ist Year	IInd Year	IIIrd Year
1.	Sex	3.27@	2.86@	4.34@
2.	Age	2.08@	1.59@	7.95@
3.	Caste	2.23@	2.97@	5.23@
4.	Exposure to Education	13.75**	0.77@	3.31@
5.	Occupation	5.79@	2.98@	4.58@
6.	Income	15.89**	5.64@	5.36@
7.	Type of Family	3.00@	2.43@	1.59@
8.	Marital Status	2.32@	0.93@	2.12@
9.	No. of Childrens	1.07@	1.53@	6.44@

@ Not significant.

** Significant at 0.01 level.

The results relating to the association between personal characteristics and retention of literacy over a period of 3 years presented in the table shows that at the end of third year the calculated chi-values between personal characteristics and retention of literacy was found to be not significant. Hence the hypothesis. "There exists no association between personal factors and retention of literacy" is accepted. It indicates that no personal characteristic has significant an association with the retention of literacy among the neo-literates. Similar trend was also found at the end of second year. However, earlier exposure to education and income of the neo-literate had association with the retention of literacy initially at the end of first year. This clearly shows that the personal characteristics of the neo-literates has not played any role in retention of literacy and need not be considered as a factor for promotion and retention of literacy activities.

Influence of Personal Characteristics in Retention of Literacy

In order to study the influence of the personal characteristics of the sample on their retention of literacy, the sample were classified into different groups based on their personal characteristics and their respective mean attainment scores in reading, writing, arithmetic and total literacy over a period of three years were calculated, and presented in the table—. Further, in order to study the role of these characteristics on all the components of literacy was also analysed. The findings are presented in four section. In section I the influence of personal characteristics on retention of reading skills over a period of three years was presented. Similarly, role of personal characteristics on the retention of writing skills, numeracy and total literacy were also presented separately in the sections II, III and IV respectively.

Section I: Influence of Personal Factors in Retention of Reading Skills

The mean reading skills attained and retained by different groups of the sample over a period of three years were presented in the table and interpreted. Further the findings revealed that the end of first year the mean reading scores obtained by the men and women sample shows that women have attained 33.48 mean reading scores and 32.23 by the men sample. This shows that women have performed better than the men. Similarly trend was retained through out the period of study. The women has improved their mean reading performance at the end of second year but lost at the end of third year. In case of men, they lost their reading skills gradually over a period three years. The difference between mean reading scores obtained by the men and women groups are not significant at the end of first and third year. However it is significantly different at the end of second year. It indicates that the difference of retention of reading skill is significantly different between men and women at the end of second year only.

In case of age, the mean retention score was found to be similar between different age groups at different intervals of time. The calculated 'F' value is an indication for the same. On the whole all the groups have lost the reading skill slightly over a period of three years. It clearly indicates that the effort made through post literacy and continuing education programmes to improve the reading skills among the target has not yielded the desired results.

Table—3.6: Personal factors vs performance in reading

Sl. No.	Character	Group	N	Ist Year			IInd Year			IIIrd Year		
				Mean	SD	t/F	Mean	SD	t/F	Mean	SD	t/F
1.	Sex	Men	800	32.25	4.84	1.39**	32.08	3.58	3.09**	30.59	4.91	2.30*
		Women	1200	33.48	3.67		34.23	3.15		33.13	4.24	
2.	Age	Young	500	32.88	4.91	0.11@	33.16	4.48	0.39@	32.08	4.19	0.07@
		Middle	700	32.77	4.08		33.08	31.4		32.14	4.97	
		Elders	800	33.22	3.58		33.75	3.20		32.47	4.60	
3.	Caste	OC	500	32.96	5.00	0.68@	32.76	3.11	0.86@	31.32	5.33	0.67@
		BC	800	32.45	3.49		33.25	2.58		32.60	3.85	
		SC/ST	700	33.60	4.29		33.94	4.25		32.54	4.84	
4.	Exposure to Education	3	580	33.72	4.01	2.74@	33.27	4.09	0.31@	32.27	5.08	0.67@
		2	380	31.00	4.52		32.89	2.61		33.32	3.41	
		1	1040	33.29	3.95		33.35	3.39		31.86	4.71	
5.	Occupation	Labour	540	32.37	4.53	1.93@	33.85	4.01	0.35@	32.74	4.95	0.49@
		Agriculture	1180	32.62	3.63		33.22	3.04		32.29	4.61	
		Housewives	380	31.43	5.25		33.07	4.07		31.21	3.95	
6.	Income	Low	740	33.37	4.27	1.44@	33.53	3.71	4.82**	32.94	4.39	4.65**
		Middle	940	32.26	4.32		32.45	3.31		30.89	4.81	
		High	420	34.00	3.59		35.19	2.72		34.29	3.52	

(Table Contd...)

1	*2*	*3*	*4*	*5*	*6*	*7*	*8*	*9*	*10*	*11*	*12*	*13*
7.	Type of family	Joint	780	33.47	3.93	0.94@	34.18	3.10	1.93@	32.68	4.47	0.73@
		Nuclear	1240	32.68	4.37		32.87	3.63		32.00	4.73	
8.	Marital Status	Married	1200	32.55	3.85	1.21@	32.95	3.35	1.47@	31.95	4.84	0.84@
		Unmarried	800	33.63	4.65		34.00	3.61		32.72	4.29	
9.	No. of children	No Child	980	32.73	4.33		33.22	3.00		32.47	4.68	
		1 Child	420	33.14	4.56	0.16@	34.19	4.63	0.75@	32.43	5.27	0.21@
		2 Child	600	33.27	3.75		33.03	3.21		31.80	4.05	

* Significant
@ Not Significant

The retention of reading skills by the sample belonging to different caste groups revealed that there is no significant difference in their retention skills at the end of first, second and third year. However, the trend of the scores revealed that there was a gradual loss of reading skill among all the caste groups over a period of three years.

The influence of the previous exposure to the education/adult education by the sample in the retention of reading skills shows that there was a loss of skill among the sample with one year and three years of exposure while there was improvement in case of sample with two years of exposure groups. However, the calculated 'F' value between different groups at the end of first, second and third year revealed that the mean retention is not significant. It indicates that their earlier exposure to education has not helped the sample to retain the reading skill.

The influence of occupation on their retention of reading skills over a period of three years among the sample revealed that there is a gradual loss of skill in all the groups and the mean difference in reading retention skills at the end of first, second and third years are found to be not significant indicating that all the groups have performed similarly.

In case of the role of income on the retention of reading skill shows that the sample with low and middle income had lost the skills in reading. However, the sample with high income groups have slightly improved the reading skills. However, the calculated 'F' – values between different income groups at the end of second and third year revealed significant difference among them. The trend of the mean retention score of reading skills revealed that the high income groups have retained more reading skills followed by low and middle income groups. It is quite natural that the high income groups are able to use the reading skills frequently in their day-to-day activities and also their frequent exposure to the reading information has helped them not only in retaining the reading skills, but also to improve upon it.

The influence of the type of family on their performance in reading at different intervals of time revealed that both the sample i.e., joint and nuclear families have lost their reading skills. The loss is maximum in case of sample from joint families. However the mean difference between these two groups are not significant at the end of first, second and third year leading to the conclusion that the mean retention rate is more or less similar in both the groups. The same trend has been exhibited by the neo-literates of different marital status and number of children groups on retention of reading skills. Further, all the groups gradually lost their skills over a period of three years.

Table—3.7: Mean retention scores in writing, SD's, t/F values obtained in the neo-literates belonging to different groups over a period 3 years

Sl. No.	Character	Group	N	Ist year			IInd year			IIIrd year		
				Mean	SD	t/F	Mean	SD	s/F	Mean	SD	t/F
1.	Sex	Men	800	19.75	3.73	2.61*	20.20	4.63	1.04@	19.32	4.81	1.89@
		Women	1200	21.83	4.16		21.08	3.32		21.00	3.53	
2.	Age	Young	500	20.48	4.92	2.23@	17.76	3.54	1.19@	10.00	3.61	2.23@
		Middle	700	20.17	4.03		21.34	4.38		20.95	4.88	
		Elders	800	22.05	3.36		20.30	3.57		21.22	3.53	
3.	Caste	OC	500	20.28	3.88	0.49@	19.88	4.46	1.67@	20.68	4.88	1.45@
		BC	800	21.25	3.65		21.57	3.32		20.95	3.08	
		SC/ST	700	21.23	4.71		20.37	3.95		19.37	4.52	
4.	Exposure to Education	3	580	21.79	4.67	3.61*	20.48	4.69	0.18@	20.10	4.13	0.15@
		2	380	18.79	2.67		20.47	3.28		20.79	3.41	
		1	1040	21.37	3.87		20.96	3.63		20.29	4.42	
5.	Occupation	Labour	540	20.78	4.78	0.36@	19.89	3.51	1.11@	21.00	4.15	0.47@
		Agriculture	1180	21.27	3.79		21.20	4.13		20.08	4.06	
		Housewives	380	202.9	3.97		20.35	3.39		20.07	4.51	
6.	Income	Low	740	21.75	4.22	10.14**	20.87	3.37	1.12@	20.87	3.98	1.39@
		Middle	940	19.32	3.75		20.19	4.43		19.59	4.61	
		High	420	23.62	2.90		21.71	3.21		21.14	2.98	

(Table Contd...)

1	2	3	4	5	6	7	8	9	10	11	12	13
7.	Type of family	Joint	780	20.82	3.78	0.36@	20.95	3.85	0.43@	20.76	4.02	0.82@
		Nuclear	1240	21.11	4.32		20.59	3.95		20.06	4.23	
8.	Marital Status	Married	1200	20.32	3.84	2.02*	20.12	3.27	1.12@	20.10	4.35	0.69@
		Unmarried	800	22.02	4.32		20.92	3.39		20.67	3.86	
9.	No. of children	No child	980	20.76	4.34		20.78	4.22		20.51	4.23	
		1 Child	420	19.26	4.07	2.99**	20.90	3.99	0.06@	21.28	4.77	1.39@
		2 Child	600	2.37	3.33		20.53	3.27		19.36	3.35	

* Significant at 0.05 level

** Significant at 0.01 level

@ Not significant

The trend of the mean reading retention scores revealed that the women, elders, SC/ST, one year exposed education, agriculturists, high income, joint family, unmarried, one child groups of neo-literates have retained and performed better than the other groups in reading skills.

Section II: Influence of Personal Characteristics on the Retention of Writing Skills

In order to study the influence of personal characteristics on the retention of writing skills among the neo literates, the sample were classified into different groups and their respective retention skills in writing were calculated. The t/F test was applied to study the difference if any among them. The results were presented in the table 3.7.

The results presented in the table 3.7 reveals that the overall writing retention skills over a period of three years was declined among all the neo-literates. Further, the difference between the mean retention scores among different groups also reveals that except few all the sub-groups have performed more or less similarly.

The retention of writing skills among the men and women neo-literates, was found to be declined. Further, the loss of retention among the women is higher than the men. However, the calculated t-test in case of first year is significant indicating that the difference in mean retention between men and women is significant. However, the difference is not significant at the end of second, third years. But women had kept an edge over men in retaining the writing skills.

In case of age, during the first year and third year the elders have retained their writing skills (21.22) followed by middle age (20.25) and young (19.00). The over-all mean differences between the three groups were not significant in all the three years leading to the conclusion that all the groups have performed similarly and the influence of age on retention of writing skills among the neo-literates is not significant. Again in case of influence of caste on the retention revealed that the mean differences among different castes is not significant in all the three years. However, during the period of the trend of the mean writing retention skills among BC and SC/STs were declined, on the other hand, the retention of writing skills has slightly increased in case of forward caste neo-literates.

The effect of earlier exposure to education on retention of writing skills was found to be not significant. Further, the mean attainment scores in retention of writing skills were found to be declined in the case of neo-literates with three years and one year of exposure to the education. On the other hand, the writing skills get strengthened in the case of the neo-literates who had two years of exposure to education.

The influence of occupation on retention of writing skills shows that there is a slight improvement in case of neo-literates with labour background and declined in the case of agriculture and households. However, the increase or decrease is not statistically significant indicating that the retention of writing skills is similar among all the groups leading to the conclusion that there is no influence of occupation in retention of writing skills.

There is a significant difference between the mean retention of writing skills among low, middle and high income groups at the end of first year. However, the mean differences are not significant at the end of second and third years. However, the high income groups has an edge over middle, and low income groups on retention of writing skills. On the whole, the low income and high income groups have lost their writing skills, whereas middle income group has improved its performance by the end of third year.

In case of joint and nuclear families, the neo-literates from nuclear families could not performed well at the end of third year. On the other hand the neo-literates from joint family also could not performed well. Further, the mean differences between these two groups is not significant leading to the conclusion that the effect of type of family is not significant. In case of married and unmarried neo-literates, there is a significant difference between the groups at the end of second year. The unmarried group has faired well than the married group. However, the married group was able to retain the skills by the end of third year and unmarried group had lost heavily.

In case of neo-literates with different number of children, indicates that one child group has improved its performance at the end of third year. Whereas the two and above children group faired badly when compared with the no child group. Further, the mean differences between the three groups is not significant.

On the whole, the mean retention skill in writing was found to be more or less similar among all the groups and there was a declining trend. This clearly indicates that the follow-up activities undertaken in the form of post-literacy and continuing education programmes are found to be not effective. Hence it is advised to promote the writing skills among the neo-literates. The neo-literates should be encouraged to use these skills regularly and for their own advantage and the programme administrators should create suitable environment and opportunity for the above.

Section—III: Influence of Personal Characteristics in Retention of Arithematics

In Order to Identify the Extent of Retention of Numeracy Skills Among the Neo-literates, A Numeracy Test was Administered Thrice at an Interval of One Year. Later, the Character and Group–wise Attainment Scores was Calculated Applied t/F Test to Study the Differential Attainment Among Different Groups.

The sex-wise retention of arithmetic skills shows that both the groups were able to retain the skills that they have attained. Further, the trend is declining from first year to third year in both the groups. The mean differences between the groups was not significant leading to the conclusion that both the groups performed similarly. In case of the age, the mean difference between young, middle and elder groups is also not significant. The trend of the mean arithmetic scores shows that there is slight improvement in the performance of numeracy in case of younger and elder neo-literates, but there is a loss of skill in the case of the neo-literates of middle aged.

The influence of the caste on the retention of numeracy skills shows no impact. However, the trend of attainment in arithmetic skills was found to be slightly improved in case of neo-literates belonging to SC/STs. However, the neo-literates among SC/STs had lost the mean difference among the different caste groups is not significant. The effect of earlier exposure to education is found to be not significant among the neo-literates in their retention of skills in numeracy.

Table—3.8: **Mean retention scores in Arithmetic SD's and t/F values obtained by the neo-literates belonging to different groups over a period of 3 years**

Sl. No.	Character	Group	N	Ist year			IInd year			III year		
				Mean	SD	t/F	Mean	SD	t/F	Mean	SD	t/F
1.	Sex	Men	800	20.87	4.29	0.86@	19.55	4.57	1.85@	20.40	4.03	1.37@
		Women	1200	21.60	3.81		21.03	2.64		21.56	4.35	
2.	Age	Young	500	21.26	4.48	0.37@	20.12	3.02	0.53@	21.72	3.38	2.21@
		Middle	700	20.94	3.91		20.14	4.34		19.65	4.72	
		Elders	800	21.72	3.78		20.90	3.17		21.97	4.00	
3.	Caste	OC	500	21.60	3.38	0.10@	20.44	3.89	0.04@	21.68	4.51	0.18@
		BC	800	21.12	3.52		20.32	3.56		21.35	3.05	
		SC/ST	700	21.31	4.89		20.57	3.69		21.11	5.15	
4.	Exposure to Education	3	580	22.62	42.1	2.63@	20.55	4.04	0.26@	21.93	4.76	1.30@
		2	380	20.50	3.05		19.89	3.65		19.89	2.85	
		1	1040	21.04	4.05		21.57	3.31		21.07	4.27	
5.	Occupation	Labour	540	21.22	5.26	2.64@	20.15	4.09	0.31@	20.78	3.53	1.51@
		Agriculture	1180	21.86	3.45		20.67	3.59		21.63	4.64	
		Housewives	380	19.14	2.79		20.00	2.42		19.50	3.39	
6.	Income	Low	740	21.97	4.13	2.21@	21.50	3.17	3.09*	21.59	4.56	4.54**
		Middle	940	20.43	4.22		19.53	3.79		19.89	3.79	
		High	420	22.28	2.83		20.85	3.31		23.05	3.91	

(Table Contd...)

1	*2*	*3*	*4*	*5*	*6*	*7*	*8*	*9*	*10*	*11*	*12*	*13*
7.	Type of Family	Joint	780	21.97	3.37	1.37@	21.08	2.84	1.51@	21.37	4.05	1.19@
		Nuclear	1240	20.90	4.33		20.05	3.96		20.71	4.35	
8.	Marital Status	Married	1200	21.33	3.88	0.07@	20.12	3.72	1.12@	20.22	3.95	2.57*
		Unmarried	800	21.27	4.24		20.29	3.39		22.42	4.37	
9.	No. of Children	No Child	980	21.92	4.12	1.21@	20.31	3.92	0.36@	20.79	4.09	0.51@
		1 Child	420	20.38	4.38		20.09	4.04		20.85	4.16	
		2 Child	600	20.97	3.42		20.90	2.59		21.76	4.53	

* Significant at 0.05 level

** Significant at 0.01 level

@ Not significant

The neo-literates with 3 years and 2 years of exposure to education had lost their skills. On the other hand, neo-literates with 1 year of exposure to education were able to retain the skill. The influence of occupation on the retention of numeracy skills revealed that the neo-literates with labour and agricultural backgrounds had lost their skills and housewives were able to improve their retention of arithmetic skills. The mean difference between the three groups was found to be not significant over a period of three years.

In case of neo-literates with different levels of income shows that the neo-literates with high income group has improved their retention of numeracy skills. On the other hand, the low and middle income groups had lost their skills. The mean differences between the three groups in retention of numeracy skills was found to be significant at the end of second and third years. The neo-literates with more income groups have performed well when compared with the other groups.

The influence of family background revealed that the neo-literates from joint families have lost more skills than the neo-literates from nuclear families. On the whole, both the groups have lost their skills. Further, the mean differences between these two groups are found to be not significant leading to the conclusion that both the groups have performed similarly.

The influence of martial status on the retention of numeracy skills revealed that there is a significant difference between the neo-literates of married and unmarried at the end of the third year. However, the trend of mean retention of numeracy skill revealed that the unmarried group has faired well than the married group.

In case of neo-literates having different number of children revealed that there is no significant difference between the two groups. Further, the trend of the mean retention scores revealed that the neo-literates with one child has improved its performance and the neo-literates with no child and two child groups could not performed well. Further, the mean differences in retention of numeracy among these three groups was found to be not significant.

On the whole, the neo-literates belonging to elders, forward caste, backward caste, one year of exposure to education, housewives, high income, unmarried, one child groups was not only retained their skill in numeracy but also improved their performance. All the other groups had lost their skills in numeracy with the passage of the time. Hence, the programme administration should take necessary steps to provide opportunities and training for the neo-literates in usage of the numeracy skills in their day to day life.

Section—IV: Influence of Personal Characteristics in Retention of Literacy

In order to study the role of personal characteristics on the retention of literacy among the neo-literates, the sample was classified into different groups and their respective mean retention scores of literacy was calculated. Further, the t/F test was applied to study the mean differences if any among different groups over a period of 3 years. The obtained results are presented in the table.

The results presented in the Table shows that in case of sex, it is noticed that both men and women have lost the literacy skill acquired initially (72.20 and 77.23) and retained only 71.24 and 75.18 mean scores respectively. Further the calculated 't' test revealed that there is a significant difference between the mean literacy scores of men and women at the end of first year and second year but the difference is not significant at the end of third year. The trend of the mean retention scores shows that women has retained more literacy than the men neo-literates.

The influence of age on retention shows that the elder new literates has retained more literacy than the other two groups viz., young and middle aged. Further the loss of skill is more or less same in all the groups. Further calculated 'F' value between different age groups is not significant. It revealed that the rate of retention is similar in all the groups.

The role of caste in retention of literacy revealed that there is loss of skill over a period of 3 years in all the groups. Further the mean differences among different caste groups is also not significant leading to the conclusion that all the caste groups retained similarly. The mean retention scores shows that neo-literates belonging to BC caste group has retained more literacy followed by SC/ST and OC groups.

Table—3.9: Mean literacy retention scores SD, obtained at the end Ist, IInd and IIIrd by the neo-literates belonging to various groups

Sl. No.	Character	Group	N	Ist year			IInd year			IIIrd year		
				Mean	SD	t/F	Mean	SD	t/F	Mean	SD	t/F
1.	Sex	Men	800	72.20	10.89	2.40*	72.20	10.60	2.18*	71.47	11.55	1.72@
		Women	1200	77.23	9.15		76.28	6.49		75.18	8.84	
2.	Age	Young	500	74.52	10.88	1.21@	72.88	8.62	0.80@	72.36	8.88	0.83@
		Middle	700	73.54	10.51		74.74	9.89		72.83	12.01	
		Elders	800	77.10	9.08		75.67	7.11		7.530	8.90	
3.	Caste	OC	500	74.28	11.29	0.36@	73.32	9.41	0.42@	782.76	10.23	0.57@
		BC	800	74.77	8.03		75.35	6.62		75.05	8.12	
		SC/ST	700	76.37	11.38		74.80	9.81		72.83	11.94	
4.	Exposure to Education	3 years	580	77.45	10.14	3.61*	74.93	10.52	0.14@	74.45	11.25	0.47@
		2 years	380	69.84	6.72		73.68	7.52		75.11	7.60	
		1 year	1040	75.92	10.58		74.85	7.74		72.76	10.28	
5.	Occupation	Labourer	540	74.59	11.91	2.19@	73.63	9.14	0.95@	73.41	01.27	0.45@
		Agriculture	1180	76.36	9.34		75.61	8.71		74.35	10.39	
		Housewives	380	70.43	8.29		72.57	6.29		71.50	7.54	
6.	Income	Low	740	76.62	9.19	5.92**	75.69	7.96	3.08*	75.25	9.57	4.11*
		Middle	940	71.94	01.76		72.55	9.61		70.83	10.99	
		High	420	80.38	7.26		77.26	5.38		77.76	6.74	

(Table Contd...)

1	2	3	4	5	6	7	8	9	10	11	12	13
7.	Type of Status	Joint	780	76.65	8.98	1.16@	76.10	6.55	9.45@	75.47	7.99	1.48@
		Nuclear	1240	74.32	10.76		73.75	9.55		72.61	11.17	
8.	Marital Status	Married	1200	73.96	9.21	1.45@	74.03	9.08	9.91@	72.35	10.91	1.72@
		Unmarried	800	97.07	11.24		75.57	7.78		75.743	8.59	
9.	No. of Children	No child	980	75.49	11.08		74.25	8.99		73.73	10.48	
		1 Child	420	72.81	10.56	0.81@	74.43	9.48	0.19@	74.28	10.54	0.06@
		2 Child	600	76.43	784		75.46	7.17		73.23	9.37	

* Significant at 0.05 level

@ Not significant

** Significant at 0.01 level

The influence of earlier exposure to education shows that neo-literates with two years of exposure has retained more literacy followed by 3 years and one year. Further the mean difference is also not significant except at the end of the first year. The occupation wise analysis shows that the loss of retention of literacy is more among the neo-literates belonging to agriculturists followed by labourers and housewives. Further the mean difference is not significant among different groups indicating that the rate of retention among different occupation groups is similar.

The results presented in the tables shows the significant role of income on the retention of literacy. The calculated 'F' value is significant at the end of the first year, second and third year. It shows that the groups are significantly differ from each other in their retention of literacy. The trend of mean retention scores shows that mean retention and loss is more in case of high income group followed by low income and middle income group. The influence of type of family on retention of literacy revealed that loss of retention among the members of nuclear families is more. On the other hand retention is more in case of joint families. Further there is no significant difference between the mean retention scores of the neo-literates belonging to joint and nuclear families. In case of marital status the loss of retention is more in case unmarried and mean difference is also not significant between them. In case of children the retention of literacy is more in case of one child group, and loss is more in case of two and more children groups. Further the loss is more in case of two and more children group. The mean difference is not significant among different groups of neo-literates.

On the whole the relationship between retention of literacy and personal characteristics of the neo-literates shows that the relationship is significant only in case of income for all the three years and sex at the end of first and second year. Hence the hypothesis. There is no significant relationship between personal factors and retention of literacy is accepted only in case of income and sex in case of first and second year only and rejected in case of other characteristics.

4

Neo-Literates Perception Towards the Programme Factors

The adult literacy programmes was designed to improve the status of the literacy among the masses assuming that the literacy will accelerate the socio-economic development of the individuals and the country as a whole. In the process of development of literacy mainly three factors are involved i.e. that the environment instructional arrangements, and administration of the programme. All the three factors put together contribute for the success of the programme. However the success of any developmental initiative largely depends on the participation of the target in it. Further the rate of participation is governed by the perception of the target towards the various aspects of the programme. Keeping in view of the above, an attempt was made in this section to study the perception of the neo-literates towards the various aspects of the programme. The knowledge about their perception will help to understand the ins and outs of the programme and it enable the programme administrators to strengthen the programme.

The neo-literates perception about the programme as measured by administering a questionnaire to the neo-literates. The responses of the neo-literates were pooled together and analysed. The response based on the personal characteristics of the neo-literates were classified and presented in the following pages.

Neo-literates Perception Towards Programme Factor

The perception of the neo-literates towards the programme factors was analysed in three stages i.e. in the first stage neo-literates perception about the environmental aspects of the programme was analysed. In the second stage the instructional aspects of the programme was studied. In the third phase the administrative aspects of programme was analysed based on the personal characteristics of the neo-literates. Finally all the above put together was considered as programme factors and analysed to bring out the trend of the perception of the neo-literates belonging to various groups towards programme as a whole.

(i) Sex Vs Programme Factors

The mean environmental perception scores of men and women neo-literates shows that the men has perceived that the programme has more congenial environment than the women neo-literates. However the calculated 'F' value shows that the mean difference is not significant indicating that both the men and women perceived the environmental equally. In view of the above the programme administrators should take steps to identify the environmental aspects that are coming in the way of women and should solve them to enhance the participation of the women in the programme.

With regard to the instructional arrangement, the women neo-literates has rated higher than the men. In other words women neo-literates felt satisfaction about the teaching learning arrangement than the men. In view of the above, the programme administration should identify the deterrents as perceived by the men and take suitable steps to improve the arrangements to make it more effective. However the calculated 'F' value revealed that there is no significant difference between the mean instructional scores of the men and women.

The perception of the neo-literates men and women towards the administrative aspects shows that men felt that the administrative aspects is more effective than the women. Further the calculated 'F' value also revealed that the difference is significant. Hence, the administrators should take suitable steps the elicit the opinion of the women towards the weak aspects of the programme and strengthen them so as to make it more convenient.

The overall perception of the men and women neo-literates shows that men neo-literates have attained more mean programme scores than women neo-literates. However the mean difference shows that it is not significantly differ from each other.

Table—4.1: Mean perception scores, SD's, t/ 'F' values obtained by different groups of neo-literates in the areas environment, instructions and administration and programme factors as a whole

Sl. No.	Character	Group	N	Environment			Instructional			Administrative			Programme factor		
				Mean	SD	Mean	Mean	SD	t/F	Mean	SD	t/F	Mean	SD	t/F
1.	Sex	Men	800	33.70	5.49	0.72@	20.97	3.78	1.11@	43.10	8.56	2.01*	97.77	12.69	1.33*
		Women	1200	32.83	6.41		21.88	4.32		39.68	7.88		94.57	10.38	
2.	Age	Young	500	33.12	5.92		21.36	3.93		40.92	9.52		94.44	13.00	
		Middle	700	33.72	5.84	0.23@	22.06	5.27	0.46@	40.54	8.16	0.14@	96.40	11.43	0.25@
		Elders	800	32.75	6.32		21.15	2.90		41.57	7.62		96.25	10.35	
3.	Caste	OC	500	31.04	5.69		21.80	4.75		40.56	6.79		93.52	11.83	
		BC	800	34.05	5.59	2.12@	21.85	4.06	0.51@	41.65	8.57	0.17@	98.12	10.58	1.42@
		SC/ST	700	33.71	6.48		20.94	3.68		40.71	8.29		94.91	11.72	
4.	Exposure	3	580	32.14	6.13		21.32	3.54		40.13	7.28		93.62	11.10	
		2	380	33.79	5.49	0.60@	19.89	3.57	2.30@	43.74	7.76	1.24@	97.42	11.44	0.81@
		1	1040	33.54	6.10		22.23	4.45		40.58	8.60		96.52	11.51	
5.	Occupation	Labourer	540	33.15	6.75		20.89	6.43		41.92	7.13		95.78	10.79	
		Agriculture	1180	32.69	5.29	1.02@	21.20	3.55	3.25*	40.38	8.19	0.22@	95.17	11.67	0.57@
		Housewives	380	35.28	4.74		24.07	6.24		40.28	10.59		98.86	11.38	
6.	Income	Low	740	32.62	6.13		21.94	4.96		40.31	8.21		93.91	11.53	
		Middle	940	34.28	5.95	1.64@	21.17	3.85	0.33@	41.57	8.54	0.21@	96.96	11.53	0.68@
		High	420	31.57	5.77		21.67	3.21		41.00	8.14		96.33	10.84	

(Table Contd...)

1	2	3	4	5	6	7	8	9	10	11	12	13	14	15	16
7.	Type of Families	Joint	780	33.45	5.92	0.35@	21.66	4.24	0.26@	39.20	8.21	1.93@	94.00	11.17	1.28@
		Nuclear	1240	33.01	6.16		21.43	4.07		42.29	8.16		96.98	11.50	
8.	Marital Status	Married	1200	33.50	5.79	0.73@	21.73	4.38	0.65@	40.35	8.10	1.20@	95.70	11.42	1.16@
		Unmarried	800	32.63	6.42		21.20	3.72		42.10	8.53		96.07	11.53	
9.	No. of Children	No Child	980	33.67	6.35		21.14	3.78		39.79	8.02		94.22	11.68	
		1 child	420	35.33	469	3.83@	22.38	5.22	0.64@	42.95	9.14	1.21@	100.47	10.53	2.21@
		2 Child	600	30.87	5.71		21.53	3.73		41.77	7.88		95.27	10.89	

@ Not significant

* Significant at 0.05 level

(ii) Age Vs Programme Factors

The mean programme factor scores obtained by the neo-literates of different age group shows that the middle age neo-literates has rated high on environment, instructional and programme factors and elders felt that administrative factors of the programme was strong. On the other hand, environmental aspects, and instructional aspects are found to be week as per the elders. Further the middle aged and young neo-literates felt low on administrative and programme factors respectively. The programme administrators should look into it and improve the programme.

(iii) Caste Vs Programme Factors

The perception of the neo-literates of various caste group shows that there is no significant difference among them on various aspects of programme and programme factors as a whole. However the trend of the mean programme aspects shows that the neo-literates belongs to forward castes has rated low on all the items and the backward castes rated high. On the other hand the SC/ST has rated it moderate. In view of the above the programme administrators should concentrate on the SC/ST to change their attitude towards the programme and elicit the cooperation from the forward castes to make the programme an effective one.

(iv) Exposure to Education Vs Programme Factors

The trend of the mean programme aspects obtained by the neo-literates with varied exposure to education revealed that there is no significant perception with regard to the environment, instructional aspects, administrative aspects and programme factors as a whole. However the trend shows that the neo-literates of two years exposure have rated more on the aspects, environment, administration and programme factors as a whole. On the other hand the one year exposure group has rated more on instructional factors. Further the one year exposure group has perceived it low in the areas of environment, administrative and programme factors. The two years exposure group has rated low on instructional aspects. In view of the above the programme administrators should take effective measures to remove the apathy towards programme among the neo-literates having some exposure to the education.

(v) Occupation Vs Programme Factors

The perception of the neo-literates of different occupational groups revealed that there is no significant difference among them about the various aspects of the programme. However the trend shows that the housewives has rated high on the aspects of environment, instructional and programme factors as a whole and the labourers has rated on high on administrative aspects of the programme. Whereas the neo-literates with agricultural background has rated low on environment, administration and programme factors. Whereas the labourers has rated low on instructional aspects. Keeping in view of the above the programme administrators should take suitable measures to improve the outlook of the programmes in the eyes of the above groups.

(vi) Income Vs Programme Factor

The neo-literates with different levels of income has perceived the programme similarly as the calculated 'F' value is not significant. In case of environment the middle income group has rated it as strong followed by low and high income groups. In case of instructional aspects more or less all the groups has rated similarly with little mean differences. The trend of the mean scores on administrative aspects revealed that the middle income group has rated high followed by high and low income groups. The programme factors as a whole the middle income group has rated high followed by low and high groups. On the whole, all the groups perceived the programme factors similarly.

(vii) Type of Family Vs Programme Factor

The trend of the obtained mean programme factors of the neo-literates of joint and nuclear families revealed the similar trend in all programme aspects. Further the 't-value' is less than the table value indicating that there is no significant difference between them. The neo-literates of joint families has rated high on environmental and instructional aspects and the other group rated high on administrative and programme factors.

(viii) The Marital Status Vs Programme Factors

The neo-literates of married and unmarried group does not differ significantly on all the programme aspects revealing that they perceive similarly. However the trend revealed that the married neo-literates has rated more on environment and instructional aspects. On the other hand the unmarried neo-literates rated high on administrative and programme factors as a whole.

(ix) Number of Children Vs Programme Factors

The findings disclosed that neo-literates of different child group does not differ significantly from each other on instructional, administrative and programme factors but they do differ significantly on environmental aspects. The neo-literates with one child group has rated high on all the programme factors. Contrary to the above the neo-literates without children has rated low on instructional, administrative and programme factors. On the other hand the neo-literates with two child group felt that the environment is weak.

Sum-up

The neo-literates belonging to women, elders, forward castes, three years of exposure to education, agriculturist, high income, nuclear families, unmarried and two child groups has rated low on environmental aspects of the programme. In case of instructional aspects, the neo-literates belonging to men, elders, SC/ST, two years of exposure to education, agriculturists, middle income, nuclear families, unmarried and no child groups has rated low. The neo-literates belonging to women, middle age, SC/ST, one year of exposure to education, housewives, low income, joint families, married and no children group has rated low on administrative aspects of the programme. The programme factors as a whole the men, young, forward caste, three years exposed, agriculturists, low income, joint families, married and no child groups of neo-literates has rated low. In view of this the programme administrators should take effective steps to improve the perception of the neo-literates towards the programme.

Influence of Programme Aspects on Retention of Literacy

In order to study the influence of the programme aspects on retention of literacy, the neo-literates were classified into three groups based on their mean programme aspects scores independently and as a whole as low, medium and high scores and calculated their respective retention scores in three components of literacy and literacy as a whole at the end of first, second and third year scores. Further 'F' test was calculated between the three groups. The findings related to the influence of programme aspects on retention of various components of literacy as a whole were presented in the following pages.

(i) *Role of Environmental Aspects in Retention of Reading Skill*

The influence of the programme environment on the retention of reading skills by the neo-literates at different intervals of time shows that the mean retention scores does not differ from low, medium and high scores on environment. It shows that all the three groups has retained literacy similarly. Further it also demonstrates that environment created for the promotion of the programme has no role in the retention of literacy by the neo-literates.

Table—4.2: Mean reading retention scores, SD values obtained by the neo-literates of low, moderate and high scores on environmental aspects

Sl. No.	Year	Low		Moderate		High		F-value
		Mean	SD	Mean	SD	Mean	SD	
1.	First Year	32.39	4.46	33.80	4.15	32.6	3.90	1.04@
2.	Second Year	33.79	3.45	33.46	3.56	32.84	3.40	0.59@
3.	Third Year	32.03	4.83	32.80	4.73	31.91	4.28	0.36@

@ Not significant

The trend of the mean retention scores obtained by the neo-literates of low environment scores shows that at the end of first year the mean retention of reading is 32.39 and increased to 33.79 at the end of second year and stabilised at 32.03 at the end of third year. In case of moderates scores, the mean retention score in reading has gradually decreased from 33.80 to 32.80. It indicates that the skill is last in course of time and more or less similar trend is also prevailed in case of high scores on environmental aspects.

(ii) *Environmental Aspects Vs Retention in Writing Skill*

The role of instructional aspects in retention of writing skills shows that there is no significant mean difference between the low, moderate and high scores on environmental aspects at the end of first year in their mean writing retention scores. The trend shows that low and high scores in environmental aspects has obtained more or less similar retention scores. It also revealed that retention in writing skill was lost during the study period.

Table—4.3: Mean writing retention scores, SD and 'F' values obtained by the neo-literates of low, moderate and high scores on environmental aspects

Sl. No.	Year	Low		Medium		High		F-value
		Mean	SD	Mean	SD	Mean	SD	
1.	First Year	21.455	3.870	20.229	3.979	21.375	4.414	0.93@
2.	Second Year	21.030	3.881	20.829	3.924	20.313	3.917	0.28@
3.	Third Year	20.061	3.969	20.829	4.539	20.063	3.897	0.37@

@ Not significant

In case of moderate scores on environmental aspects their retention in writing skill has not changed significantly but slightly improved in the second year and stabilised at the end of third year at the same level. On the whole influence of environmental aspects on retention of writing skill was found to be not significant.

(iii) Environmental Aspects Vs Retention in Arithmetic

The trend of the obtained mean retention scores in arithmetic by the low, moderate and high scores on environment aspects of the programme shows that the low scores has increased in their retention. On the other hand the moderate scores has lost the skills. In case of high scores they have retained their writing skills. The mean differences between these three groups at the end of first, second and third year shows that there is no significant difference among them. It indicates that the role of the environmental aspects of the programme was found to be not significant in writing skills.

Table—4.4: Mean arithmetic retention scores obtained, SD values obtained by the neo-literates of low, moderate and high scores on environmental aspects

Sl. No.	Year	Low		Medium		High		F-value
		Mean	SD	Mean	SD	Mean	SD	
1.	First Year	20.242	4.120	21.971	3.821	20.656	4.015	0.88@
2.	Second Year	20.606	4.199	20.086	3.698	20.656	2.734	0.25@
3.	Third Year	21.364	3.796	21.286	4.151	20.625	4.781	0.28@

@ Not significant

(iv) *Environmental Aspects Vs Retention in Literacy*

The mean literacy retention scores obtained by the neo-literates of different scores on environmental aspects revealed that there is no significant difference among them at the end of first, second and third year. The calculated 'F' value was found to be lower than the table value. It indicates that low, moderate and high environmental groups has retained their literacy skill more or less similarly. Further it implies that environmental aspects of the programme has no role in the retention of skills. However the trend of the mean retention scores obtained by the low, moderate and high scores in environmental aspects has lost their literacy skills in the study period. In view of this, it is necessary that the programme administrators should take necessary steps to help the neo-literates to retain the literacy skill by creating conducive environment.

Table—4.5: Mean literacy retention scores SD values obtained by the neo-literates of low, moderate and high scores on environmental aspects

Sl. No.	Year	Low		Medium		High		F-value
		Mean	SD	Mean	SD	Mean	SD	
1.	First Year	75.697	10.934	75.229	10.198	74.688	9.319	0.07@
2.	Second Year	75.606	8.011	74.200	9.208	74.156	8.471	0.29@
3.	Third Year	73.121	9.435	74.857	10.787	73.031	10.135	0.34@

@ Not significant

Sum-up

The influence of the environmental aspects of the programme on the future retention of the components of literacy and literacy as a whole was found to be not contributing. In addition it is also observed that the retention in writing skill was found to be decreased over a period of three years. In view of this, it can be concluded that the environment created during the programme period could not be sustained during the post programme period. As a result, the skills that has been obtained by the neo-literates could not be retained due to lack of educative environment. Hence the programme administrators should take appropriate measures to retain the writing skills among the neo-literates.

Role of Instructional Arrangements in Retention of Literacy

In order to identify the influence of instructional arrangements made during the programme period on the retention of literacy, the neo-literates were classified into three groups as low, moderate and high scores on instructional arrangements and their respective mean retention scores in reading, writing, arithmetic and literacy as a whole at the end of first, second and third year was calculated. Further 'F' test was applied to study the mean differences if any among the neo-literates of the above groups. The findings of the above analysis are presented in the following pages.

(i) *Instructional Arrangements Vs Retention in Reading*

The trend of the reading retention scores presented in the Table shows that the neo-literates with low scores and moderate scores has lost their reading skills over a period of three years. On the other hand the high scores group on instructional aspects has not only retained the skills but also improved. However the mean differences between low, moderate and high scoring groups of neo-literates on instructional aspects does not differ from each other at end of first, second and third year. It clearly demonstrates that the instructional arrangements made during the programme has no future role in retaining the reading skills among the neo-literates.

(ii) *Instructional Arrangements Vs Retention in Writing*

The mean retention in writing scores of the neo-literates with low, moderate and high scoring in instructional arrangements at the end of first, second and third year shows that the low and moderate group has lost the retention of the writing skills. On the other hand the high scoring groups on instructional arrangements was found to be improved in their retention of writing skills over a period of three years. In addition the 'F' value calculated between the three scoring groups on instructional arrangements at the end of first, second and third year shows that there is a significant difference at the end of first year and the difference is not significant at the end of second and third year. The findings reveals that the role of instructional arrangements made during the programme period was found to be not significant in retention of writing skills after the programme period.

Table—4.6: Mean retention scores in literacy SD's and 'F' value obtained by the low, moderate and high scores in the area of the instructional aspects over a period of three years

Sl. No.	Year	Low		Medium		High		F-value
		Mean	SD	Mean	SD	Mean	SD	
Mean Reading Retention Scores								
1.	First Year	33.03	4.54	33.81	3.129	32.11	4.59	1.35@
2.	Second Year	33.30	3.71	33.33	3.19	33.47	3.55	0.02@
3.	Third Year	31.60	4.29	31.98	5.00	33.17	3.77	1.04@
Mean Writing Retention Scores								
1.	First Year	22.12	4.42	21.36	3.95	19.55	3.54	3.55@
2.	Second Year	20.84	4.00	20.57	4.21	20.76	3.51	0.04@
3.	Third Year	20.60	4.80	19.90	3.82	20.47	3.78	0.25@
Mean Arithmetic Retention Scores								
1.	First Year	21.81	4.18	21.51	3.82	20.61	3.98	0.79@
2.	Second Year	20.93	4.20	20.21	2.78	20.17	3.85	0.46@
3.	Third Year	20.24	3.93	21.60	4.36	20.47	4.39	0.60@
Mean Literacy Retention Scores								
1.	First Year	77.09	12.39	76.48	7.66	72.14	9.20	2.40@
2.	Second Year	75.09	9.98	74.63	7.89	74.23	7.79	0.08@
3.	Third Year	73.30	10.76	72.97	11.05	74.79	8.49	0.29@

@ Not significant

(iii) Instructional Aspects Vs Retention in Arithmetic

The role of instructional aspects of the programme on the future retention of arithmetic skills among neo-literates shows that there is no significant improvement of retention over a period of three years. Further the mean differences between the neo-literates of low, moderate and high scores on instructional aspects was found to be not significant over a period of three years. This shows that the instructional aspects of the programme in nothing to do with the future retention skills among the neo-literates in writing.

(iv) Instructional Aspects Vs Retention in Literacy

The contribution of instructional aspects of the programme for the future retention of the literacy among the neo-literates for a period of three years shows that there is no significant difference between the high, moderate and low scores in their retention of literacy skills. Further the retention skills among the low and moderate scores are found to be last over a period of three years. Contrary to the above, the high scores have not only retained the skills but also improved in their literacy skills.

Sum-up

The instructional aspects of the programme on retention of literacy skills shows that it has no significant role. But it is also found that the low and moderate scores in instructional aspects has lost their skills and the high scores has gained the skills over a period of three years.

Table—4.7: Mean retention scores in literacy, SD's and 'F' values obtained by the low, moderate and high scores in the area of administrative aspects of the programme over a period of three years

Sl. No.	Year	Low		Medium		High		F-value
		Mean	SD	Mean	SD	Mean	SD	
Mean Reading Retention Scores								
1.	First Year	33.36	3.61	32.89	4.6	32.79	3.94	0.13@
2.	Second Year	33.64	32.7	31.71	3.84	34.17	2.92	1.64@
3.	Third Year	32.68	3.72	31.54	5.02	33.03	4.56	1.04@
Mean Writing Retention Scores								
1.	First Year	21.40	3.48	20.87	4.67	20.86	3.65	0.15@
2.	Second Year	20.80	2.49	20.08	4.83	21.69	2.98	1.49@
3.	Third Year	20.04	3.81	20.34	4.90	20.55	3.03	0.09@
Mean Arithmetic Retention Scores								
1.	First Year	20.96	3.53	21.17	4.43	21.82	3.68	0.35@
2.	Second Year	20.76	3.17	20.30	3.95	20.37	3.37	0.13@
3.	Third Year	21.08	4.22	20.71	4.74	21.72	3.34	0.48@
Mean Literacy Retention Scores								
1.	First Year	75.68	7.30	74.78	4.31	78.48	8.42	0.097@
2.	Second Year	75.16	6.01	74.41	10.87	76.17	5.70	0.96@
3.	Third Year	74.60	9.20	72.45	11.82	74.89	7.63	0.60@

@ Not significant

4. Administrative Aspects Vs Retention of Literacy

In order to bring out role of administrative aspects of the programme on the retention of literacy among the neo-literates, the selected sample neo-literates were classified into three groups as low, moderate and high scorer groups and their respective mean retention scores on literacy was calculated and 'F' test was applied to study the mean differences if any among them. The analysis of the results are presented in the table.

(i) Administrative Aspects Vs Retention in Reading Skill

The trend of the mean retention scores in reading shows that the low and moderate scores in administrative aspects of the programme has lost their reading skills over a period of three years. On the other hand, the high scores has not only retained their literacy skills but also improved in their performance in reading. The calculated 'F' values between low, moderate and high scores shows that they were not differ from each other significantly. It indicates that irrespective of the administrative scores, all the neo-literates performed similarly in reading skills.

(ii) Administrative aspects Vs Retention in Writing Skills

The influence of administrative aspects of the programme on retention of the writing skills among the neo-literates shows that their is no significant difference between the low, moderate and high scoring groups of neo-literates in their retention in writing skills. Further the trend also shows that in all the groups, the retention was found to be low and it is losing.

(iii) Administrative Aspects Vs Retention in Arithmetic

The retention scores in arithmetic obtained by different groups of neo-literates shows that there is no significant difference between the low, moderate and high scoring groups on administrative aspects in their retention in arithmetic. This also implies that administrative aspects of the programme does not have any role in their retention. The trend also shows that more are less in all the groups has performed similarly through out the study period. Hence it is suggested that administrative strategies adopted during the literacy programme may not be helpful in retaining the skills after the programme.

(iv) Administrative Aspects Vs Retention in Literacy

The mean retention literacy scores obtained by the neo-literates of low, medium and high scores on administrative aspects shows that there is no significant difference between them. In other words all the three groups has performed similarly throughout the study period. Further the trend also shows that literacy which was acquired initially could not be retained during the study period but also lost some skill during the period.

Sum-up

The role of administrative aspects of the programme was found to be not reflected in the retention of literacy. Further it was found that the literacy skills attained by the neo-literates was retained with marginal loss over a period of three years. This should be kept in view while formulating the post-literacy and continuing education programmes so as to enhance the changes of retention and promotion of literacy skills.

Role of Programme Factors on Retention of Literacy

In order to study the role of programme factors as a whole on the retention of literacy skills the neo-literates were categorised into three groups as low, moderate and high scoring groups on programme factors and their respective retention of literacy scores was calculated. The 'F' test was applied to study the differences if any among them and presented the findings in the table 4.8.

(i) Programme Factors Vs Retention in Reading

The trend of the mean retention scores obtained by the neo-literates shows that there is no significant difference between low, moderate and high scoring groups of neo-literates. Further the retention of reading scores over a period of 3 years shows that the neo-literates tends to loose their skill during the study period. In other words the contribution of programme factors for retention of reading skills among the neo-literates was found to be low.

(ii) Programme Factors Vs Retention in Writing

The role of programme factors as whole on retention of writing skill was found to be not significant as the 'F' values obtained between low, moderate and high scoring groups are found to be lower than the table value. Further the trend of the mean retention scores in writing over a period of 3 years shows that there is minor loss of skills in al the groups.

In other words, the role of programme factors are found to be losing its influence over a period of time in their capacity in retaining the writing skills.

(iii) Programme Factors Vs Retention in Arithmetic

The influence of the programme factors on the retention of the Arithmetic skills among the neo-literates shows that there is no significant difference between the low, moderate and high scores on programme factors in their mean retention scores in writing. On the other hand, the retention skill over a period of 3 years shows that their performance was in case of low and moderate scores on programme factors and retained at the same level by the high scores. On the whole it appears that the programme factors as a whole does not have significant role in retention of arithmetic skills.

(iv) Programme Factors Vs Retention in Literacy

The mean literacy retention scores obtained by the neo-literates of low, moderate and high scoring groups on programme factors shows that all the three groups attained lower retention scores after three years of time. In other words some of the skills originally acquired was lost in course of time. Further the calculated 'F' values between the three groups of neo-literates also shows that they does not differ each other in their retention of literacy scores. It shows that programme factors has no significant role in retention of literacy among the neo-literates. Hence the hypothesis, there is no significant influence of the programme (environment, instruction and administrative factors on retention of literacy" is accepted.

Table—4.8: Mean retention scores in literacy, SD's and 'F' values obtained by the low, moderate and high scores of programme factors over a period of 3 years

Sl. No.	Yes	Low		Medium		High		F-value
		Mean	SD	Mean	SD	Mean	SD	
Mean Reading Retention Scores								
1.	First Year	32.80	4.24	33.23	3.91	32.94	4.38	0.19@
2.	Second Year	33.14	3.63	33.20	3.57	33.74	3.24	0.30@
3.	Third Year	31.91	4.73	32.03	5.00	32.80	4.16	0.36@

(Table Contd...)

Mean Writing Retention Scores								
1.	First Year	21.31	3.71	21.00	4.25	20.68	4.38	0.19@
2.	Second Year	20.34	4.10	20.86	4.11	21.00	3.50	0.26@
3.	Third Year	20.48	4.36	19.73	4.58	20.68	3.49	0.44@
Mean Arithmetic Retention Scores								
1.	First Year	20.77	3.76	22.30	4.12	21.00	4.05	1.31@
2.	Second Year	20.22	3.33	20.53	3.86	20.57	3.65	0.09@
3.	Third Year	21.37	33.9	20.90	4.72	21.00	4.61	0.11@
Mean Literacy Retention Scores								
1.	First Year	75.00	9.41	76.30	10.87	74.48	10.24	0.26@
2.	Second Year	74.25	8.53	74.50	9.92	75.17	7.38	0.10@
3.	Third Year	73.34	9.27	72.80	13.06	74.82	7.85	0.34@

@ Not significant

Sum-up

The role of programme factors on retention of literacy shows that there is no significant difference between the low, moderate and high scores on programme factors on their retention of skills in reading, writing, arithmetic and literacy as a whole. Further it appears that the literacy attainment over a period of three years at an interval of one year shows that gradually the literacy was tend to loose due to lack of practical application.

Role of Programme Factors on Socio-economic Development

In order to study the role of programme factors in socio-economic development among the neo-literates, the neo-literates were classified into three groups based on their scores on different programme aspect as low, medium and high scores. The mean socio, economic and socio-economic development scores obtained by the different scores on programme aspects was calculated. Further 'F' test was applied to study the differences if any among all programme aspects and programme factors as a whole.

(i) *Role of Environmental Aspects on Socio-Economic Development of the Neo-literates*

The analysis of relationship between environmental aspects and socio-economic and socio-economic development as a whole over a period of three years are presented in the table.

The results presented in the table shows that there is no significant difference between low, medium and high scores on environmental aspects in their social development over a period of three years. Further there exists a growth of social development among low and moderate group of scores in environmental aspects. However the social development was slightly decreased at the end of third year among the high scores.

The role of environmental factors on economic development shows that there is no significant difference between the three scoring groups in their economic development. However the trend shows that economic development is growth oriented and has increased in all three groups. In other words irrespective of environment aspects, there was a economic development among all the groups in view of the possession of literacy.

The socio-economic development as a whole, among the neo-literates over a period of three years shows that there was a growth in all the three groups of neo-literates. Further the growth is maximum in case of low and medium scores on environmental aspects. It also indicates that difference between mean socio-economic development scores obtained by the low, medium and high scores are found to be not significant. It indicates that irrespective of the environment scores, there was a socio-economic development among the neo-literates. The growth is similar in all the groups.

Table—4.9: Mean scores, SD's obtained at the end of Ist, IInd and IIIrd year by the low, medium and more scores on environmental aspects by the neo-literates along with 'F' value on social, economic and socio-economic development

Sl. No.	Programme Aspect	Year	Environmental Aspects						
			Low		Medium		High		F-value
			Mean	SD	Mean	SD	Mean	SD	
1.	Social develop-ment	First Year	32.80	4.24	33.23	3.91	32.94	4.38	0.19
		Second Year	33.14	3.63	33.20	3.57	33.74	3.24	0.30
		Third Year	31.91	4.73	32.03	5.00	32.80	4.16	0.36
2.	Economic develop-ment	First Year	17.33	3.78	18.20	3.54	16.97	3.39	0.93@
		Second Year	18.00	2.76	17.97	3.62	17.72	4.69	0.05@
		Third Year	18.06	3.19	18.97	3.64	18.15	4.09	0.62@
3.	Socio-Economic develop-ment	First Year	67.64	17.19	65.28	13.99	67.06	14.71	0.21@
		Second Year	69.36	17.73	65.34	13.36	66.00	13.21	0.68@
		Third Year	72.73	17.38	71.49	14.42	69.12	16.71	0.40@

@ Not significant

(ii) Role of Instructional Aspects on Socio-economic Development of the Neo-literates

The obtained mean social development score by the low, medium and high scores on instructional aspects over a period of three years shows that there is no significant difference among the above three groups in their social development. It is also evident that the calculated 'F' values are lower than the table values. However the trend of the social development scores shows that it has increased in all the three groups. The growth is maximum in case of medium scores followed by low scores and high scores.

Table—4.10: Mean scores, SD's obtained at the end of Ist, IInd and IIIrd year by the low, medium and more scores on Instructional aspects by the neo-literates along with 'F' value on social, economic and socio-economic development

Sl. No.	Programme Aspect	Year	Instructional Aspects						F-value
			Low		Medium		High		
			Mean	SD	Mean	SD	Mean	SD	
1.	Social Develop-ment	First Year	49.03	14.08	48.09	16.55	50.47	14.44	0.21@
		Second Year	50.39	12.89	49.79	16.89	46.26	11.43	0.84@
		Third Year	52.27	16.24	54.18	17.29	51.06	12.57	0.34@
2.	Economic Develop-ment	First Year	17.76	4.47	17.18	2.98	17.61	3.72	0.20@
		Second Year	17.58	3.39	18.27	4.23	17.85	3.59	0.27@
		Third Year	18.69	3.35	18.33	3.56	18.21	4.05	0.15@
3.	Socio-Economic develop-ment	First Year	66.48	14.08	65.27	16.15	68.09	15.68	0.27@
		Second Year	691.5	15.96	67.91	16.26	63.67	11.93	1.22@
		Third Year	71.8	15.96	72.39	18.12	69.21	14.30	0.36@

@ Not significant

The economic development attained by the neo-literates shows that it is growth oriented and has increased over a period of three years in all the groups. However the mean socio-economic development scores among low, medium and high scores on instructional aspects shows that the difference is not significant indicating that all the three groups performed similarly and also the role of instructional aspects on economic development of the neo-literates is not significant.

In case of socio-economic development as a whole the performance of the low, medium and high scores on instructional aspects was found to be similar at the end of first, second and third year. All the three groups recorded, the socio-economic development over a period of three years. Among them the growth is more among low score followed by medium and high scores. It indicates that the instructional aspects of the programme is nothing to do with the socio-economic development of the neo-literates.

(iii) Role of Administrative Aspects on Socio-economic Development of the Neo-literates

The trend of the mean social development scores obtained by low, moderate and high scores on administrative aspects shows that there is no significant difference among them in their social development scores at the end of first, second and third years. Further the trend of the social development scores shows that it is growth oriented and increased over a period of three years among all the three groups. It is more in the case of moderate scores followed by high and low scores.

In case of economic development the obtained mean economic development scores by the low, moderate and high scores revealed that there is a significant difference among them at the end of first, second and third year indicating that there is a significant difference among them. The trend of the mean scores shows that high scores on administrative aspects has attained more economic development scores followed by moderate and high scores. In other words higher the administrative scores higher the economic development. Further the economic development was also increased during the study period.

Table—4.11: Mean scores, SD's obtained at the end of Ist, IInd and IIIrd year by the low, medium and more scores on Administrative aspects by the neo-literates along with 'F' value on social, economic and socio-economic development

Sl. No.	Programme Aspect	Year	Administrative Aspects						F-value
			High		Moderate		Low		
			Mean	SD	Mean	SD	Mean	SD	
1.	Social development	First Year	53.84	14.72	47.00	13.33	48.72	17.03	1.69@
		Second Year	50.96	16.27	47.56	11.18	48.86	15.66	0.46@
		Third Year	54.56	16.97	51.26	14.52	52.65	15.49	0.36@
2.	Economic development	First Year	19.60	4.04	17.11	3.55	16.38	3.17	5.83**
		Second Year	20.16	4.38	17.26	3.28	16.97	3.05	6.68**
		Third Year	20.40	3.25	17.91	3.53	17.48	3.65	5.38**
3.	Socio economic development	First Year	73.04	14.11	64.11	13.03	65.10	18.06	3.02@
		Second Year	70.72	15.67	65.58	13.45	65.62	16.15	1.08@
		Third Year	76.12	16.28	69.22	15.25	69.89	16.86	1.582

** Significant at 0.01

@ Not significant

When the socio-economic development was taken as a whole the growth was recorded in case of all the groups namely high, moderate and low scores. However the difference among the three groups was not significant. Further it indicates that all the three groups has performed similarly.

(iv) Role of Programme Factors on Socio-economic Development of the Neo-literates

The mean social development scores obtained by the low, moderate and high scores on programme factors shows that there was a growth in social development among all the groups of neo-literates. The growth is more in case of moderate scores followed by low and high scores on programme factors. Further the calculated f-value shows that there is no significant difference between the socio-economic development scores among the low, moderate and high scores on programme factors.

The mean economic development scores obtained by the neo-literates of low, moderate and high scoring groups on programme factors shows that there is a significant difference among them. The moderate scores has attained more economic development followed by low and high scores. There is a growth of economic development among all the groups. The growth is more in case of high scores followed by moderate and low scores.

Table—4.12: Mean development scores, SD's obtained at the end of Ist, IInd and IIIrd year by the low, medium and more scores on Programme factors by the neo-literates along with 'F' value on social, economic and socio-economic development

Sl No.	Programme Aspect	Year	Programme Factors						F-value
			High		Moderate		Low		
			Mean	SD	Mean	SD	Mean	SD	
1.	Social develop-ment	First Year	50.14	14.49	47.06	13.67	50.11	16.58	0.42@
		Second Year	49.40	13.97	48.33	13.18	48.57	14.74	0.05@
		Third Year	52.86	17.26	52.00	14.54	52.54	14.41	0.02@
2.	Economic develop-ment	First Year	17.60	4.35	18.80	3.04	16.34	3.52	3.56*
		Second Year	17.80	3.54	19.23	4.25	16.86	3.14	3.35*
		Third Year	18.51	3.59	19.53	3.47	17.34	3.63	2.96@
3.	Socio economic develop-ment	First Year	67.45	14.05	65.86	13.94	66.45	17.61	0.08@
		Second Year	68.17	16.52	68.06	19.4	64.57	14.00	0.63@
		Third Yeai	72.29	17.25	71.30	16.01	69.86	15.30	0.19@

* Significant at 0.05

@ Not significant

The trend of the mean socio-economic development scores obtained by the neo-literates of low, moderate and high scoring groups on programme factors shows that there is no significant difference among them at the end of first, second and third years. On the other hand it has recorded the growth in all the three cases. The growth is maximum in case of moderate scores followed by low scores and high scores.

5

Literacy and Change in Socio-economic Status

Realising the potentiality of the literacy in accelerating pace of socio-economic development, the Government of India has launched a number of literacy programmes to improve the literacy percentage among the masses especially in the age group of 15-35 years. The District Total Literacy campaigns launched under the aegis of National Literacy Mission is a significant milestones in the history of literacy movement in India. As a part of the above, the districts in the Rayalaseema region of Andhra Pradesh also launched the total literacy campaigns and all the districts crossed the total literacy, post literacy phases and entered into the third phase i.e. the continuing education. In order to study the influence of literacy in socio-economic development of the neo-literates over a period of three years, an index was developed. The socio-economic index was administered to the selected neo-literates at the end of the first year, second year and third year. The mean socio-economic development scores was calculated for all the three years and 'F' test was applied to study the mean difference if any. Further the role of personal characteristics of the neo-literates in their social, economic and socio-economic status was also studied.

Growth of Socio-economic Development Among the Neo-literates

In order to study the impact of literacy on the socio-economic development of the neo-literates, those neo-literates who has acquired literacy through total literacy programme i.e. after one year of internal evaluation has chosen. The socio-economic development index was administered 3 times at on interval of one year. The growth of the neo-literates in terms of social, economic and socio-economic status was presented in the following pages.

(i) Social Development Among the Neo-literates

The social development of an individual was measured based on his interaction with fellow beings, official participation in the community activities such as membership in the local groups, societies, and in the programmes implemented for their benefit by the government etc. The social development index was administered to the selected sample and the mean social development scores are calculated and presented in the table.

Table—5.1: Mean social developmental scores, SDs, 'F' values obtained by the sample over a period of 3 years

Sl. No.	Year (At the end of)	Social Development		'F' value
		Mean	SD	
1.	First Year	49.21	15.09	
2.	Second Year	48.79	14.03	1.83@
3.	Third Year	52.49	15.51	

@ Not significant

The trend of the social development of the neo-literates over a period of 3 years shows increasing trend. At the end first year the mean social development score is 49.21 and it has gone down to 48.79 at the end of second year and later grown to 52.49. The calculated 'F' value is less than table value indicating that the social development among neo-literates is more or less similar during the 3 years of period. However there is a net growth of social development among the neo-literates.

(ii) Economic Development Among Neo-literates

The mean economic development scores obtained by the neo-literates over a period of 3 years presented in the table shows that the economic development of the neo-literates was measured based on the index developed for the purpose. The items included in index ranged from availability of modern domestic gadgets, type of house, rooms available, facilities provided in the house, landed property, gold etc. The cumulative index of the economic development of the neo-literates are presented in the Table.

Table—5.2: Mean economic development scores, SDs, 'F' value obtained by the sample over a period of 3 years

Sl. No.	Year (at the end of)	Economic Development		'F' value
		Mean	SD	
1.	First Year	17.52	3.78	
2.	Second Year	17.90	3.77	1.40@
3.	Third Year	18.41	3.68	

@ Not significant

The economic development of the neo-literates after acquiring literacy over a period of 3 years presented in the table shows that there is marked growth of economic development. The economic growth is marginal between first and second year (0.39) and improved between second and third year (0.51). However the calculated 'F' value is not significant indicating that the growth of economic development is similar.

(iii) Socio-economic Development

The socio-economic development scores of the neo-literates presented in the table shows that the socio-economic development is improved over a period of three years. The socio-economic development between first and second year, it is only 0.25 points. Whereas the growth between second and third year it is 4.26 points. It shows the rapid growth of economic development during the period.

Table—5.3: Mean social economic development scores, SD, 'F' values obtained by the sample over a period of 3 years

Sl. No.	Year (At the end of)	Socio-economic Development		'F' value
		Mean	SD	
1.	First Year	86.63	15.37	
2.	Second Year	86.88	15.01	2.63@
3.	Third Year	91.14	16.25	

@ Not significant

However the calculated 'F' value shows that relationship between literacy. The trend shows that after acquiring literacy the socio-economic development will start after one year stabilises in the second year and quickens the pace after second year. Hence, this may be kept in view while motivating the target for the adult literacy programmes.

The above analysis relating to the social, economic and socio-economic development of the neo-literates over a period of 3 years revealed that there is a growth of socio-economic development of the neo-literates between first and second year is very slow. But pace of growth has increased between second and third year. This should be kept in view while formulating and implementing the literacy programmes.

Influence of Personal Characteristics on Social Development

In order to study the influence of personal factors on the social development of the neo-literates over a period of three years, the sample neo-literates are classified into different groups. The social development scores of these groups of neo-literates are calculated and applied the 't'/F test to study the mean difference if any among different groups of neo-literates. The details of the analysis and obtained values are presented in the table 5.3.

(i) Sex Vs Social Development

The trend of the obtained mean social development scores of men and women shows that social development was found to be more in case of women than the men neo-literates over a period of 3 years. However there is also a considerable growth of social development among men. The calculated 't' value also shows that it is significant at the end of second year and not significant at the end of Ist and IIIrd year. The social development among women was found to be more. Hence effects should made to help the women to retain the tempo in future.

(ii) Age Vs Social Development

The mean social development scores obtained by different age groups shows that there is a constant increase of social development in all the age groups. Further the social development is similar in all the age groups as the calculated 'F' values are less than table values. In spite of all these, the trend clearly revealed that the social development is more in case of middle age neo-literates followed by elders and young. In view of this, the programme administrations should take suitable steps to encourage the young to utilise the literacy in their day to day life to improve their social status.

(iii) Caste Vs Social Development

The influence of the caste on social development among the neo-literates shows that, the social development is more in case of neo-literates belonging to SC/ST followed by forward castes and backward castes. However at the end of first year there is more social development among backward castes followed by SC/ST and forward castes. At the end of second year it is forward castes, where there is more growth than the other groups. By the end of third year, the SC/ST reached the peak followed by forward castes and backward castes. The calculated 'F' values shows that the difference of growth is not significant. It indicates that more or less there is a similar growth among all the groups.

(iv) Exposure to Education Vs Social Development

The role of earlier exposure to the education in the social development of the neo-literates revealed that the growth is more in case one year of exposure to education followed by 3 years and two years. The mean social development is not significantly differ between different groups. However the growth of social development is visible in all the groups.

(v) Occupation Vs Social Development

The growth of social development was found in all the occupational groups. Further the growth is more in case of agriculturists followed by labourers and least in case of housewives. Further the calculated 'F' value was found to be not significant between different occupations and groups indicating that they does not differ from each other significantly. In view of the above, the housewives should be encouraged to use the literacy skills in their day to day life to improve their status in the society.

(vi) Income Vs Social Development

To analyse the role of income of the neo-literates on their social status, the social development scores of the three income groups are calculated and 'F' test was applied. The trend of the mean social development scores shows that growth is high among the high income groups followed by low income group. The growth is least in case of middle income group. However the calculated 'F' value is not significant. It shows that the social development is more or less same in case of all the groups. The low income group of neo-literates should be encouraged to use the literacy skills to improve their income leading to the growth in social development.

(vii) Type of Family Vs Social Development

The trend of the mean social development scores obtained by the neo-literates of joint and nuclear families shows that they does not differ from each other in their social development. However it also reveals that the noe-literates from nuclear families were able to use literacy for their social development effectively.

(viii) Marital Status Vs Social Development

The role of marital status on social development shows that there is a growth of social development among married and unmarried neo-literates. However the growth was found to be more in case of unmarried neo-literates than the married. But the calculated 't' value revealed that the difference in the mean social development scores was found to be not significant indicating that both the groups has performed similarly. The married neo-literates especially the women should be encouraged to use the literacy to empower themselves to utilise the opportunities created for their development by the Government.

(ix) No. of Children Vs Social Development

The influence of the children on the social development of the neo-literates shows that social development is more in case of no child groups followed by one child group. Further it also revealed that social development is low in case of the neo-literates with 2 and more children. Further the calculated 'F' value revealed that the mean difference is significant only at the end of third year. It shows that the mean social development is significantly difference from each other and social development is more in case of no child group. It appears that other groups may not be using the literacy in their day to day life and hence should be advised to use it for their own development.

The role of the personal characteristics on the social development shows that, the social development is more in case of women, middle aged, SC/ST, one year of exposure to education, agriculturists, high/income, nuclear families, unmarried and no child groups. On the other hand social development is low in case of men, young, BC, two years of exposed groups. Hence efforts should be made to motivate the above groups to use the literacy for their social development.

Table—5.4: Mean, SDs, t/F values obtained by the end of Ist, IInd and IIIrd year by the different groups of neo-literates in their social development

Sl. No.	Character	Group	N	Ist Year			IInd Year			IIIrd Year		
				Mean	SD	t/F	Mean	SD	t/F	Mean	SD	t/F
1.	Sex	Men	800	48.25	13.56	0.54@	45.10	12.57	2.26*	49.85	12.71	1.48@
		Women	1200	49.85	16.00		51.25	14.40		54.25	16.89	
2.	Age	Young	500	49.24	16.33		47.92	15.71		51.48	18.74	
		Middle	700	48.85	12.57	0.02@	48.88	12.66	0.06@	52.85	12.53	0.07@
		Elders	800	49.50	16.25		49.25	14.02		52.80	15.60	
3.	Caste	OC	500	48.40	18.21		50.48	16.71		52.60	17.17	
		BC	800	50.17	13.02	0.14@	48.10	12.06	0.34@	51.70	15.74	0.10@
		SC/ST	700	48.68	14.78		48.11	13.87		53.31	13.85	
4.	Exposure	3	580	46.21	13.25		47.14	12.29		49.24	13.46	
		2	380	47.37	16.88	1.34@	45.00	10.49	1.60@	49.84	15.22	1.75@
		1	1040	51.56	14.98		51.09	15.55		55.26	16.14	
5.	Occupation	Labourer	540	52.92	16.68		52.0	14.51		56.03	18.28	
		Agriculture	1180	46.62	14.07	2.13@	46.91	13.66	1.33@	50.4	13.28	1.42@
		Housewives	380	52.39	13.69		50.50	13.22		54.71	15.56	

(Table Contd...)

1	2	3	4	5	6	7	8	9	10	11	12	13
		Low	740	49.96	14.05		50.93	14.01		54.47	16.57	
6.	Income	Middle	940	49.87	5.79	0.39@	41.59	12.79	1.08@	51.36	14.89	0.38@
		High	420	46.57	14.74		50.43	15.86		52.00	14.92	
7.	Type of Status	Joint	780	48.21	15.19	0.51@	46.76	10.77	1.23@	50.55	13.55	1.03@
		Nuclear	1240	49.28	15.00		50.30	15.56		53.68	16.48	
8.	Matiral Status	Married	1200	49.13	14.73	0.06@	48.00	13.47	0.69@	50.93	16.21	1.27@
		Unmarried	800	49.32	15.62		49.97	14.61		54.28	14.07	
		No child	980	48.63	16.17		48.08	14.91		53.08	16.60	
9.	No. of Children	1 Child	420	54.95	15.22	22.1@	53.38	14.56	15.1@	58.85	13.42	3.81*
		2 Child	600	46.13	11.69		46.37	11.15		47.06	12.93	

* Significant

@ Not significant

Influence of Personal Characteristics on Economic Development

In order to study the role of personal characteristics on economic development, after acquiring the literacy, the neo-literates were classified into different groups and calculated their respective mean economic development scores and applied the 'F' test to study the significant differences if any among. The details of the analysis and obtained values are presented in the table.

(i) Sex Vs Economic Development

The trend of the economic development scores obtained by the neo-literates over a period of three years shows that there is marked improvement of economic development. The growth is more (1.22) among the women than the men (0.76). However the mean difference between men and women in their economic development is not significant. It indicates that the growth of economic development is similar among both the groups.

(ii) Age Vs Economic Development

The economic development among different age groups of neo-literates shows that there was a growth of development during the study period. The growth is more in case of middle aged and it is similar in case of young and elders at the end of third year. The calculated 'F' value shows that the difference between the three groups are found to be not significantly differ from each other in all the three years. At the end of first year the growth is similar among middle aged and older. However it is low in case of young. However at the end of second year, the growth is more in case of elders followed by young and middle aged. Middle aged attained maximum growth followed by elders and young at the end of third year.

(iii) Caste Vs Economic Development

The influence of the caste on the economic development of neo-literates shows that it is more in case of SC/ST followed by backward caste and forward castes at the end of first year. The same trend was prevailed at the end of second and third year also. However, the calculated 'F' value revealed that the difference between the different caste groups are found to be significant at the end of second year only. It indicates that the growth is more or less similar in all the groups at the end of first and third year. However the mean growth rate during the study period shows that it is more in case of backward castes followed by forward caste and SC/ST neo-literates.

(iv) *Exposure to Education Vs Economic Development*

The role of earlier exposure to education of the neo-literates on their economic development shows that the neo-literates with two years of exposure has attained more growth followed by 3 years of exposure and 1 year of exposure at the end of first year. However at the end of second year the neo-literates with 3 years of exposure has attained more growth followed by one year and two years of exposure. In case of third year the neo-literates with two years of exposure have attained more growth followed by three years and one year exposure. However the results of the ANOVA reveals that the growth of economic development does not differ from each other. In other words all the three groups performed similarly.

(v) *Occupation Vs Economic Development*

The trend of the mean economic development scores obtained by the neo-literates belongs to different occupation groups shows that the growth of economic development is similar in all the groups and it is growth oriented. Further the 'F' test also revealed that the mean difference is not significant between different groups. All the occupational groups performed more or less similarly.

(vi) *Income Vs Economic Development*

The economic development is more in case of middle income group followed by high and low income groups at the end of first year. At the end of second year the growth is low in case of low income group and similar in case of middle and high income group. Further the growth is more in case of high income group followed by middle and low income group at the end of third year. The calculated 'F' value also revealed that the growth is similar in all the groups.

(vii) *Type of Family Vs Economic Development*

The neo-literates from nuclear families has attained more economic growth than the joint families at the end of first year. Further there is a marked growth of economic development among both the groups during the study period. The economic growth among nuclear families is 0.73 mean points where as in case of joint families it is 1.14 mean points by the of third year.

(viii) Marital Status Vs Economic Development

The trend of the mean economic development of the married and unmarried neo-literates shows that there is no significance between them. The economic development is more in case of unmarried neo literates than the married literates during the study period.

(ix) No of Children Vs Economic Development

The role of children on the economic development shows that the neo-literates with one child has attained more economic growth followed by no child and two child group.

The influence of personal variables on economic development shows that growth of economic development is more among women, middle aged, forward caste, one year of exposure, labour, low income, nuclear families, unmarried, two child group. However the economic growth is low in case of men, middle aged, SC/ST, three years of experience, agriculture, high income, joint family, unmarried and one child group of neo-literates.

Influence of Personal Characteristics on Socio-economic Development

Recognising that in addition to the literacy, the personal characteristics of the neo-literates also plays a role in their socio-economic development, the neo-literates were classified into different groups based on their personal characteristics and their respective socio-economic development scores were calculated. Further t/F test was applied to study the differences if any among the and presented in the table.

(i) Sex Vs Socio-Economic Development

The trend of the obtained socio-economic development scores shows that there is a marked growth among both the sex groups. The growth rate is more in case of women. The mean socio-economic development score between men and women was found to be not significant at the end of first year and third year. However the difference is significant at the end of second year. Indicating that men and women differ significantly from each other in their socio-economic development at the end of second year only.

Table—5.5: Mean SDs, t/F values obtained by the end of Ist, IInd and IIIrd year by the different groups of neo-literates in their economic development

Sl. No.	Character	Group	N	Ist Year			IInd Year			IIIrd Year		
				Mean	SD	t/F	Mean	SD	t/F	Mean	SD	t/F
1.	Sex	Men	800	17.59	4.20	0.89@	18.00	4.27	0.20@	18.35	3.57	0.13@
		Women	1200	17.23	3.45		17.83	3.39		18.45	3.75	
2.	Age	Young	500	16.84	3.83		17.92	4.61		17.44	4.12	
		Middle	700	17.74	4.08	0.52@	17.60	3.28	0.192	19.14	3.27	1.56@
		Elders	800	17.75	3.41		18.15	3.54		18.37	3.58	
3.	Caste	OC	500	17.08	5.09		17.20	3.67		17.92	3.89	
		BC	800	17.47	2.96	0.32@	17.50	3.11	3.67*	18.50	3.62	0.31@
		SC/ST	700	17.88	3.49		18.85	4.28		18.66	3.54	
4.	Exposure to education	3 Years	580	17.48	3.41		18.00	3.43		18.21	3.69	
		2 Years	380	18.74	4.59	1.31@	17.79	3.51	0.012@	19.47	3.63	0.97@
		1 Year	1040	17.09	3.54		17.88	4.02		18.13	3.61	
5.	Occupation	Labourers	540	17.56	3.44		58.59	4.19		18.22	3.91	
		Agriculture	1180	17.47	3.39	0.01@	17.69	3.50	0.64@	18.56	3.72	0.12@
		Housewives	380	17.64	5.50		17.42	3.46		18.44	2.92	

(Table Contd...)

1	*2*	*3*	*4*	*5*	*6*	*7*	*8*	*9*	*10*	*11*	*12*	*13*
		Low	740	16.50	3.10		17.06	2.46		18.21	3.28	
6.	Income	Middle	940	18.08	3.91	1.75@	18.36	4.06	1.18@	18.49	3.71	0.06@
		High	420	17.81	4.10		18.14	4.37		18.52	4.12	
7.	Type of family	Joint	780	17.28	3.48	0.49@	18.00	3.23	0.222	18.42	3.45	0.02@
		Nuclear	1240	17.67	3.95		17.84	4.06		18.40	3.81	
8.	Marital status	Married	1200	17.53	3.80	0.09@	18.13	3.85	0.78@	18.10	13.69	1.04@
		Unmarried	800	17.50	3.75		17.55	3.60		18.87	3.61	
		No Child	980	17.35	3.37		18.08	3.91		18.12	3.59	
9.	No. of	1 Child	420	17.86	4.02	0.13@	18.38	3.37	0.64@	19.00	3.74	0.41@
	Children	2 Child	600	17.57	4.21		17.26	3.69		18.47	3.72	

* Significant

@ Not significant

(ii) Age Vs Socio-economic Development

The influence of age on the socio-economic development shows that there is a mark growth among all the age groups. However the growth is more in the case of middle age followed by young and elders. Further the calculated 'F' value shows that the mean difference among different age groups was found to be not significant. It reveals that the growth is more or less similar in all the groups.

(iii) Caste Vs Socio-economic Development

The growth of socio-economic development among different caste groups shows that the growth is more in case of forward castes followed by SC/ST and least in case of backward caste. Further the mean difference between the caste groups were found to be not significant indicating that the growth is not significantly differ from each other.

(iv) Exposure to Education Vs Socio-economic Development

The influence of earlier exposure to education on socio-economic development shows that the growth rate is more in case of three years of exposure followed by one year and two years of exposure groups. The overall trend revealed that there is a growth in all the groups. However the calculated 'F' value revealed that there is no significant difference between the neo-literates with different levels of exposure to formal education.

(v) Occupation Vs Socio-economic Development

The neo-literates belongs to agricultural occupation have gained more socio-economic development followed by labourers and housewives. Further the trend also revealed growth of socio-economic development among all the groups. The 'F' values calculated at the end of first, second and third years shows that there is no significant difference between different groups indicating that all the groups have performed similarly.

(vi) Income Vs Socio-economic Development

The role of income on socio-economic development on neo-literates shows that there is a growth in all the groups. The growth is more in case of low income groups followed by high income groups. However the socio-economic growth is low in case of middle income group. However the ANOVA test revealed that there is no significant difference between mean socio-economic development scores obtained by the different income groups.

(vii) Type of Family Vs Socio-economic Development

The influence of type of family on the socio-economic development revealed that the growth is more in the case of neo-literates belonging to nuclear families. The calculated 'F' value revealed that there is no significant difference between the mean socio-economic development scores obtained by the neo-literates belongs to joint and nuclear families.

(viii) Marital Status Vs Socio Economic Development

The influence of marital status on the socio-economic development revealed that there is a marked growth of socio-economic development among married and unmarried neo-literates. However the growth is more in case of unmarried neo-literates. The results also revealed that there is no significant difference between the mean development scores obtained by the married and unmarried neo-literates.

(ix) Number of Children Vs Socio-economic Development

The trend of the mean socio-economic development scores revealed that there is a marked improvement of socio-economic development among the neo-literates with no children group followed by one child and two child groups. The 'F' value calculated at the end of third year was found to be significant, indicating that there is a significant difference between the neo-literates with different number of children. The one child group has attained more socio-economic development scores followed by no child and one child group. At the end of first year and second year the 'F' value is not significant.

The trend of the mean socio-economic development scores shows that women, middle aged, forward castes, one year exposed to education, agriculturists, low income, nuclear families, unmarried, one child groups has attained more socio-economic development than the other groups. Further it was also observed that there is a significant relationship between sex at the second year and no of children at the end of third year with the socio-economic development of the neo-literates. Hence the hypothesis "There is no significant relationship between personal factors and socio-economic development" is not accepted only in the above two cases and accepted in case of other variables.

Table—5.6: Mean SDs, t/F values obtained at the end of Ist, IInd and IIIrd year by the different groups of neo-literates in their socio-economic development

Sl. No.	Character	Group	N	Ist Year			IInd Year			IIIrd Year		
				Mean	SD	t/F	Mean	SD	t/F	Mean	SD	t/F
1.	Sex	Men	800	65.95	13.26	0.38@	63.20	13.21	2.11*	68.50	13.83	1.64@
		Women	1200	67.08	16.62		69.33	15.62		73.20	17.37	
2.	Age	Young	500	66.08	17.25	0.05@	65.68	16.87	0.28@	70.0	19.88	0.09@
		Middle	700	66.31	13.04		66.17	12.89		71.88	13.01	
		Elders	800	67.25	15.98		68.25	15.38		71.20	16.22	
3.	Caste	OC	500	65.08	18.48	0.21@	67.36	15.61	0.01@	72.52	17.25	0.24@
		BC	800	67.65	13.27		66.75	15.67		69.80	16.63	
		SC/ST	700	66.57	5.06		66.69	13.74		71.68	14.89	
4.	Exposure to education	3 Years	580	63.69	14.49	1.01@	64.66	13.18	1.03@	68.82	14.46	0.75@
		2 Years	380	65.57	17.03		64.58	16.54		69.42	15.99	
		1 Year	1040	68.65	14.91		68.96	15.07		73.50	17.02	
5.	Occupation	Labourer	540	70.48	17.02	1.97@	72.03	17.83	2.59@	74.25	20.64	0.72@
		Agriculture	1180	64.10	14.11		64.25	12.99		69.69	13.65	
		Housewives	380	69.85	14.98		68.00	14.21		72.21	15.79	

(Table Contd...)

1	2	3	4	5	6	7	8	9	10	11	12	13
		Low	740	66.47	15.48		67.75	15.02		74.15	16.72	
6.	Income	Middle	940	67.74	15.51	0.34@	65.95	15.82	0.16@	69.81	16.12	0.80@
		High	420	64.38	14.64		67.62	12.86		69.52	15.12	
7.	Type of families	Joint	780	65.50	15.31	0.58@	65.68	14.33	0.63@	68.78	14.47	1.19@
		Nuclear	1240	67.32	15.37		67.61	15.37		72.58	13.25	
8.	Marital status	Married	1200	66.50	15.05	0.10@	66.60	15.48	0.23@	69.90	17.56	0.98@
		Unmarried	800	66.82	15.89		67.30	14.26		73.00	13.84	
		No Child	980	65.98	16.76		66.53	16.71		71.12	18.04	
9.	No. of	1 Child	420	72.81	15.71	2.46@	71.81	14.43	1.71@	77.71	13.71	2.99*
	children	2 Child	600	63.36	10.86		64.00	11.13		66.57	12.85	

* Significant at 0.55

@ Not significant

6

Correlation Among Literacy, Programme Factors and Socio-economic Development

The adult literacy programmes are being implemented to inculcate the literacy among the masses to improve their socio-economic conditions. In order to attain the objectives of developing literacy and retaining the same needs suitable and also the educative environment to motivate and to attract the illiterate to attain literacy and also help them to utilise the same in their day-to-day life. In addition as the target is adults, requires a separate strategy and package of literacy instruction so as to enable them to acquire the literacy in a easiest and happiest way without any drudgery. Further in order to coordinate the field and programme planners require efficient administration. In other words the promotion of aspects of literacy leads not only for the development of literacy but also retain the same. In addition the possession of literacy also helps an individual to thin and act in a intelligible manner and depending on the situation. Keeping in view of the above, an attempt was to study the correlation if any among literacy, programme factors and socio-economic development.

Correlation Between Programme Factors and Socio-economic Development

The adult literacy programmes are designed not only to promote literacy among the neo-literates, but also the functionality and awareness among the neo-literates. The development of the functionality and awareness of the neo-literates aimed at improving the occupational skills leading to more production, resulting in increased income. In other words, the functionality was incorporated to improve the economic status of the neo-literates. In case of awareness, it is intended to help the neo-literates to know his status in the society in relation to others and to enhance his capabilities and communication skills. It is assumed that the participation of the neo-literates in various speares of life and activities of the communities includes his social status. Keeping in view of the above an attempt was made in this section to study the correlation between programme factors and socio, economic and socio-economic development among the neo-literates if any. The findings relating to the above are presented in the following pages.

(i) Correlation Between Programme Factors and Social Development

The correlation scores obtained between various programme aspects and social development of the neo-literates shows that there is a significant correlation between environment and social development at the end of third year only. It indicates that the environment created for the programme will influence the social development very slowly.

Table—6.1: Correlation between programme factors and social development

Sl. No.	Programme Factor	Social Development		
		First Year	Second Year	Third Year
1.	Environment	-0.01@	0.01@	0.13**
2.	Instruction	-0.06*	0.09**	0.04@
3.	Administrative	0.07*	0.05@	0.02@
4.	Programme factors	0.02@	0.06*	0.05@

@ Not significant

* Significant at 0.05 level

** Significant at 0.01 level

The correlation between instructional arrangement and social development was significantly correlation during first and second years only. However, the correlation was found to be not significant at the end of third year. It shows that instructional arrangements made for the programme will have immediate effect on the social development of the neo-literates and looses after second year.

The influence of administrative aspects of the programmes on social development shows that it is significantly correlated at the end of first year and not significant at the end of second year and third years indicating that the correlation between the above gradually disappears. The programme factors as a whole was significantly correlated only at the end of second year and not significant at the end of first and third years. On the whole, it appears that the correlation was not significant between programme factors and social development of the neo-literates.

(ii) Correlation Between Programme Factors and Economic Development

The correlation between programme factors and economic development of the neo-literates presented in the Table reveal that the correlation is significant in case of economic development and programme aspects viz., administrative aspects and programme factors as a whole at the end of first year. Whereas at the end of second year, the obtained 'r' value was found to be significant except in case of environment indicating that environment of the programme has no role in the economic development of the neo-literates.

Table—6.2: Correlation between programme factors and economic development

Sl. No.	Programme Factor	Economic Development		
		First Year	Second Year	Third Year
1.	Environment	0.01@	0.01@	-0.04@
2.	Instruction	-0.04@	-0.06*	-0.01@
3.	Administrative	0.29**	0.26**	0.28**
4.	Programme factors	0.23**	0.16**	0.21**

@ Not significant

* Significant 0.05 level

** Significant at 0.01 level

The correlation between the economic development of the neo-literates and programme factors revealed that the correlation is significant in case of administrative aspects and programme factors as a whole. On the whole, it can be concluded that the economic development of the neo-literates largely depends on administrative aspects of the programme and programme factors as a whole. Hence, it is suggested that while implementing the programme, the programme administrators should take effective measures to improve the economic development of the neo-literates by strengthening the administrative aspects and programme factors as a whole.

(iii) Correlation Between Programme Factors and Socio-economic Development of the Neo-literates

Table—6.3: Correlation between programme factors and socio-economic development

Sl. No.	Programme Aspects	Socio-economic Development		
		First Year	Second Year	Third Year
1.	Environment	-0.02@	0.06*	0.07*
2.	Instruction	-0.07@	0.12**	0.06*
3.	Administrative	0.13**	0.12**	0.12**
4.	Programme factors	0.06*	0.14**	0.11**

@ Not significant
* Significant at 0.05 level
** Significant at 0.01 level

The obtained 'r' values between socio-economic development and programme aspects shows that there is a correlation between socio-economic development of the neo-literates and environment and instructional arrangements of the programme at the end of second and third years, but the correlation is not significant at the end of first year. Whereas, the correlation between socio-economic development of the neo-literates and administrative aspects and programme aspects as a whole was found to be significant throughout the study period. There is a clear indication that the programme aspects individually and as a whole has a significant role in socio-economic development of the neo-literates. Hence, for promotion of socio-economic development, it is necessary that the programme factors should be very effective or otherwise, the socio-economic development will not take place among the neo-literates.

Sum-up

The correlation shows that the programme factors have very little role in social development. In case of economic developments the administrative aspects and the programme factors as a whole has a bearing on economic development of the neo-literates. As a whole, all the programme aspects are significantly correlated with Socio-Economic Development.

Correlation Between Literacy and Socio-economic Development

In order to find out the correlation between literacy and socio-economic development, the attainment of neo-literates in reading, writing, arithmetic and literacy was calculated. Further the correlation between components of literacy and social development, economic development and socio-economic development was calculated for the sample of the end of first year, second year and third year. The calculated 'r' values of the above was presented in the Table.

The calculated 'r' value between the components of literacy and socio-economic development presented in the table shows that the correlation is significant between reading and economic development. Further the correlation between the literacy components of writing, arithmetic and literacy as a whole and social development, economic development and socio-economic development at the end of first year was significant. The correlation clearly demonstrates that the literacy components has a bearing on the socio-economic development of the neo-literates.

In case of second year, the correlation was found to be significant in case of economic development and all components of literacy. Further the correlation also found to be not significant between arithmetic and social development but correlation was significant in case of other components of literacy and social development. The correlation between socio-economic development is significant in case of reading and literacy alone and not significant in case of writing and arithmetic.

The correlation between various components of literacy and social development and socio-economic development was found to be significant except in case of literacy as a whole. On the other hand the correlation was significant between economic development and writing, arithmetic and literacy but not significant between reading and economic development at the end of third year. Hence the hypothesis "There is no significant correlation between the relation of literacy and socio-economic development" was accepted in case of reading at the end of first year, writing and arithmetic at the end of second year and literacy at the end of third year and not accepted in rest of the cases.

The trend of the correlation shows that the literacy components and socio, economic and socio-economic development was found to be significant except in few cases. It proves that literacy has bearing on the social, economic and socio-economic development. Hence, the programme administrator should take steps to popularise in the above among the masses and motivate them to acquire the literacy.

Table—6.4: Correlation between retention of literacy and socio-economic development at end of first, second and third year along with the level of significance

Sl. No.	Components of Literacy	Socio-economic Development		
		Social Development	Economic Development	Socio-economic Development
A.	*First Year*			
1.	Reading	0.01@	0.06*	0.01@
2.	Writing	0.14**	-0.15**	-0.16**
3.	Arithmetic	-0.12**	-0.14**	-0.15**
4.	Literacy	-0.12**	-0.13**	-0.15**
B.	*Second Year*			
1.	Reading	0.21**	0.11**	0.25**
2.	Writing	0.11**	-0.16**	0.05@
3.	Arithmetic	0.01@	-0.09**	-0.02@
4.	Literacy	0.08**	-0.09**	0.06*
C.	*Third Year*			
1.	Reading	0.10**	-0.03@	0.09**
2.	Writing	0.13**	-0.08**	0.11**
3.	Arithmetic	-0.09**	-0.11**	-0.11**
4.	Literacy	0.04@	-0.07*	0.03@

@ Not significant
* Significant at 0.05 level
** Significant at 0.01 level

Correlation Between Programme Factors and Retention of Literacy

The quality and success of adult literacy programme largely lies in its attainment of the short term and long term objectives of the programme.

The long term objective of the adult literacy programme is not only to help the neo-literates to use the literacy skills, but also to retain and promote the literacy. In order to attain the above, the programme has its own in built capacity to attain the above through various programme aspects. In case of adult education, the major aspects of the programme are environment, instruction and administrative aspects of the programme. Keeping in view of the above, and to study the impact of the above on the retention of literacy, correlation scores was calculated between programme aspects and components of literacy. The obtained correlation scores between the components of literacy and programme aspects are presented in the table.

The correlation between various programme aspects and retention of components of literacy shows that the correlation between environment of the programme and retention of the arithmetic and literacy as a whole were found to be significant only at the end of the first year. However, in other cases, the environment was not correlated with the various components of literacy and literacy as a whole during the study period. The results indicates the environment has some bearing at the end of first year (arithmetic and literacy) and subsequently the environment has last it role in retention of literacy.

The correlation between the instructional arrangements made for the programme and the retention of reading, writing, arithmetic and literacy as a whole demonstrates that at the end of first year, the correlation was significant. It indicates that the instruction provided during the programme period has significantly correlated with the retention of literacy. However, in case of second year, the correlation between instruction and literacy retention as a whole was only significant and it was not significant in case of various components of literacy. Surprisingly at the end of third year, the correlation between reading, writing arithmetic and instructional arrangements are significantly correlated. But, the correlation between instruction and literacy as a whole was found to be not significant. The trend of the correlation indicates that the impact of instruction provided at the programme period gradually losses its identity in relation of literacy.

In case of the role of administrative aspects of the programme on retention of literacy, at the end of the first year shows that it is significant only in case of retention of arithmetic skill. Where as in case of second year it is significant in reading, writing and literacy as a whole. However, the results also shows that the correlation is not significant between the

Table—6.5: Correlation between programme factors and retention of literacy at the end of the first, second and third years along with the level of significance

Sl. No.	Programme Aspects	Reading			Writing			Arithmetic			Literacy		
		First Year	Second Year	Third Year	First Year	Second Year	Third Year	First Year	Second Year	Third Year	First Year	Second Year	Third Year
1.	Environment	0.02@	0.021@	-0.01@	0.01	0.05@	0.01@	0.11**	0.02@	0.05@	0.08**	0.05@	0.06*
2.	Instruction	0.1**	-0.03@	-0.15**	0.18**	0.05@	0.11**	0.08**	0.01@	0.07*	0.17**	0.06*	0.03@
3.	Administrative	-0.03@	-0.10**	-0.00	0.01	-0.09**	0.00@	-0.10**	0.01@	-0.05@	-0.05@	-0.06*	0.01@
4.	Programme Factors	0.01@	-0.07*	-0.07*	0.07*	-0.02@	0.05*	-0.05@	0.02@	0.02@	0.02@	-0.02@	0.02@

@ Not significant

* Significant at 0.05 level

** Significant at 0.01 level

administrative aspects and retention of various components of literacy and literacy as a whole at the end of the third year.

The programme factors as a whole were significantly correlated in case of reading at the end of second and third year and writing at the end of first year. The results clearly demonstrates that the programme factors as a whole has a little role in retention of various components of literacy and literacy as a whole. Keeping this in view it is suggested that the programme administration should take suitable programme measures only during literacy period and its impact on subsequent period will not be there. Hence, the administrator should identify the factors that are contributing for the literacy retention and strengthen those factors so as to enable the neo-literates to retain the literacy skills for a longer period and use them for their own development.

7

Summary and Conclusions

Recognising the influence of literacy on socio-economic status of the people, the Government of India has launched several formal and non-formal education programmes for promoting and developing literacy among various groups. The National Literacy Mission is one such attempts for promotion of literacy among the 15 to 35 years of age groups. No doubt the NLM has raised the literacy level in the country but the earlier experience of adult education programmes revealed that one of the reasons for their failure is lack of effective follow up programmes to retain the literacy and to make use of it for improving their social status. The NLM while launching the Total Literacy Campaign has taken all the steps not only to promote literacy, but to strengthen it through post-literacy programmes and created opportunities for using it practically in their day-to-day life. In other words, the success of the programme lies in retention of literacy and its effect on their socio-economic development. Hence it is necessary to study the above to know to what extent it has achieved the objective for which it was launched.

Keeping in view of the above, the present study was formulated to study the extent of retention of literacy over a period of 3 years in Rayalaseema region of Andhra Pradesh and to measure the socio-economic development of the sample during the above period. Further it is also aimed to study the role of personal variables and programme factors in retention of literacy and socio-economic development. To be specific the objectives of the study are as follows.

Objectives of the Study

1. To identify the level of retention of literacy among neo-literacy over a period of 3 years.
2. To study the impact of programme factors on the socio-economic development of the neo-literates over a period of three years.
3. To study the influence of programme factors (environment, instruction and administrative aspects) and personal factors of neo-literates on the retention of literacy.
4. To study the nature of relationship among the retention of literacy socio-economic development and programme factors.
5. To identify and study the influence of personal factors on socio-economic development and retention of literacy among neo-literates.

Hypothesis of the Study

1. The level of retention of literacy over a period of three years is not similar.
2. There exists no association between personal factors and retention of literacy.
3. There exists no significant relation between personal factors and retention of literacy.
4. There is no significant influence of programme factors on retention of literacy.
5. There is no significant association between personal factors and socio-economic development.
6. There is no significant relationship between personal factors and socio-economic development.
7. There exists no significant influence of retention of literacy on socio-economic development among neo-literates.
8. There is no significant correlation between retention of literacy programme factors and socio-economic development.

Methodology

The study was conducted in the Rayalaseema region of Andhra Pradesh. The region has 4 districts. Ten mandals were selected randomly from each district and 10 villages from each mandal and from each village 5 neo-literates were selected randomly as sample of the study. Thus the sample of the study includes, 4 districts, 40 mandals, 400 villages, 2000 neo-literates and 100 field functionaries. For the purpose of data collection, the investigator has developed an achievement test in literacy, a schedule to measure the programme factors and a tool to measure the socio-economic development of the neo-literates. The tools were administered to the selected sample thrice at an interval of one year. Thus the data was collected thrice from the same sample. However where ever same sample is not available. The sample with similar characteristics was substituted. The collected data was pooled and analysed based on the objectives of the study. The findings of the study were given below.

Findings of the Study

1. The literacy rate of Andhra Pradesh according to 2001 census is 61.11 per cent. The male and female literacy rates are 70.85 and 51.17 per cent respectively. The rural and urban literacy rate is 55.33 per cent and 76.39 per cent respectively.
2. The literacy rate in Rayalaseema is 60.65 per cent. The district wise literacy shows that Chittoor attained highest literacy with 67.46 per cent followed by Kadapa (64.02), Anantapur (56.69) and Kurnool (54.43).
3. The profile of the selected sample of the study shows that majority of them are women, elders, backward castes, literates of adult literacy programme, agriculturists, middle income group, nuclear families, married, no children groups.
4. The mean retention scores of the sample shows that the retention in reading, writing, arithmetic and literacy as a whole has slightly lost in the course of three years.
5. The association between personal factors and retention in reading was not significant. However there is a significant association between sex, caste and number of children with the retention of writing skills. In case of arithmetic and literacy as a whole it is not significantly associated with personal characteristics of the sample.

6. The sample belonging to women, elders, SC/ST, 1 year exposure to education, agriculturists, high income, joint family, unmarried, one child group of neo-literates retained and performed better than the other groups in reading skills. The study was also found that there is no significant relationship with the personal characteristics and retention of reading skills except in case of sex and income at the end of second and third year with the retention of reading skill.
7. The relationship between retention in writing skills and personal characteristics shows that sex, exposure to education, income, marital status and number of children are closely associated at the end of first year only. However such relationships was not visible at the end of second and third year. On the whole the mean retention skill in writing was found to be more or less similar among all the groups.
8. The influence of personal characteristics on retention of arithmetic skills shows that income and marital status was found to be significantly related at the end of third year and income at the end of second year with the retention of arithmetic skills.
9. There is a significant relationship between retention of literacy and sex, exposure to education and income of the sample at the end of first year, sex and income at the end of second year, income at the end of third year.
10. The perception of the neo-literate towards environmental aspects of the programme shows that women elders forward castes, three years of exposure to education, agriculturist, high income, nuclear families unmarried, two children groups of neo-literates have rated low on environmental aspects of the programme.
11. The noe-literates belonging to men, elders, SC/ST, two years of exposure to education, agriculturists, middle income, nuclear families unmarried and no child group have rated low on the instructional aspects of the programme.
12. In case of administrative aspects of the programme, the neo-literates belonging to women, middle aged SC/ST, one year of exposure to education, housewives, low income, joint families, married and no child group has rated low.

13. The programme factors as a whole the men, young, forwards, caste, three years of exposure to education, agriculturists, low income, joint families, married and no child groups of neo-literates has rated low.

14. The influence of the environmental aspects of the programme on the future retention of the components of the literacy and literacy as a whole was found to be not contributing.

15. The instructional aspects of the programme on retention of the literacy skills shows that it has no significant role but it is found that the low, moderate scores on instructional aspects has lost their skills and the high scores has gained the skills over a period of three years.

16. The role of administrative aspects of the programme was found to be not reflected in the retention of literacy. Further it was found that the literacy skills attained by the neo-literates was retained with marginal loss over a period of three years.

17. The programme factors as a whole was found to have no significant role in retention of literacy among the neo-literates in all components of literacy. Further it appears that literacy attainment over a period of three years at an interval of one year shows that gradually the literacy was tend to loss due to lack of practical application.

18. Socio-economic development among the low moderate high scoring groups on programme factors shows that there is no significant difference among them at the end of the first, second and third year. Further there was a growth in socio-economic status among all the three groups.

19. Social, economic and socio-economic development of the neo-literates between first and second year is very slow. But the pace of growth has increased between second and third year.

20. The role of the personal characteristics on the social development shows that the social development is more in case of women, middle aged, SC/ST, one year of exposed to education, agriculturists, high income, nuclear families, unmarried and no child groups. On the other hand the social development is low in case of men, young, BC, two years of exposed groups.

21. The influence of personal variables on economic development shows that growth of economic development is more among women, middle aged, forward caste, one year of exposure, labour, low income, nuclear families, unmarried, two child group. However the economic growth is low in case of men, middle aged, SC/ST, three years of experienced, agriculturists, high income, joint family, unmarried and no child group of neo-literates.

22. The women, middle aged, forward caste, one year exposure to education, agriculturist, low income, nuclear families, unmarried, one child groups of neo-literates has attained more socio-economic development.

23. The correlations shows that the programme aspects has little role in social development. In case of economic development it is found that administrative aspects and programme factors as a whole closely correlated. Further all the programme aspects are significantly correlated with socio-economic development.

24. The correlation between components of literacy, social, economic and socio-economic development shows that there is a significant correlation between three components of literacy and social, economic and socio-economic development. However literacy as a whole is correlated with economic development only.

25. The correlation between programme factors and literacy was found to be significant only with environmental aspects.

Bibliography

narayana Reddy, P. (1985) "*A Study of the Reading Preferences and Study Habits of the Neo-literates*", Experiments in Education. Vol. XIII (5) July pp. 84-90.

Ahmed Mustaq (1958); *An Evaluation of Reading Materials for Neo-literates and a Study of Their Reading Needs and Interests*, New Delhi: Research, Training and Production Centre, Jamia Millia Islamia.

Ahmed Mustaq (1985); *A Study of Relationship Between the Period of Learning and Level of Literacy and Reading Interest of New Literates*. New Delhi: Indian Adult Education Association.

Ahmed, Mustaq (1957) *Survey of Reading Materials for Neo-literates in India*, New Delhi: Indian Adult Education Association.

Aikara (1984) *Adult Education in Maharashtra: An Appraisal*, Bombay: Tata Institute of Social Sciences.

Anil Bhatt (1993), *Evaluation of Literacy Campaign*, Tumkur District, Ahmedabad: Indian Institute of Management.

Asha (1972) *Educational Needs of Rural Mothers of Children Under 5 Years of Age in Selected 9 Aspects of Child Nutrition*, Master Thesis, M.S. University.

Backer G.S (1964) *Human Capital*, New York: Columbia University Press.

Bastian L R and J E Ross (1962) *Mass Media and Wisconsin Farm Families"* Wisconsin Agri. Exp. Sta. Research Bulletin 234.

Bazony M (1971) *"Results of Achievements Tests"* Literacy Discussion 2 (2), Spring 1971, pp. 185-187.

Centre for Media Studies (1994), *Evaluation of Literacy Campaign Panipat,* New Delhi: Centre for Media Studies.

Council for Social Development (1993), *Evaluation of Literacy Campaign Karim Nagar District*, Hyderabad: CSD.

Denzil Saldanha (1992), *Evaluation of Total Literacy Campaign of Wardha District*, Bombay: Tata Institute of Social Sciences.

Denzil Saldanha (1992), *The Total Literacy Campaign in Sindhu Durg District: A Report of the Evaluation*, Bombay: TISS.

Desh Pande (1993), *Evaluation of Literacy Campaign, Jalna,* Pune: State Resource Centre.

Edward AL (1969), *Statistical Analysis,* New York: Holt, Rinehrt a Winston Inc.

Fligel (1967) *Agricultural Innovations in Indian Villages,* Hyderabad: National Institute of Community Development.

Gokul O. Parekh (1994), *Evaluation of the Literacy Campaign of Vadodara District,* Ahmedabad: Sardar Patel Institute of Economic and Social Change.

Golden H H (1955) *"Literacy and Social Change in Under Developed Countries",* Rural Sociology, XX, 1959, Reported in H.M Phillips, Literacy and Development, Paris, 1971, p. 21.

Gopala Krishna Reddy and Others (1993), *Evaluation of Literacy Campaign Vishakhapatnam District*, Vishakhapatnam: Andhra University.

Govt. of India (1986), *National Policy on Education*, New Delhi: Ministry of Human Resource Development.

Govt. of India (1988), *National Literacy Mission,* New Delhi, Ministry of Human Resource Development.

Govt of India (1995), *Evaluation of Literacy Campaigns,* Summary, Vol. II, New Delhi: Ministry of Human Resource Development.

Govt. of India (1995), *Evaluation of Literacy Campaign*, Summary Report Vol. I, New Delhi: Ministry of Human Resource Development.

Harbison F and Myers C A (1964), *Education: Manpower and Economic Growth*, New York, McGraw Hill Book Company.

Harihar, R and Rao (1982), *Adult Education in Rajasthan,* Third Appraisal (Jhunjhunu District, Ahmedabad, Indian Institute of Management).

IIALM (1977), *A Study of Reader Interest and Preference in 8 Iranian Villages,* Tehran: International Institute for Adult Literacy Methods.

Indradeva (1993), *Evaluation of Literacy Campaign Rajpur,* Ravi Shankar University.

Institute of Social Science (1993), *Evaluation of Literacy Campaign,* Goa, Bangalore: Institute of Social Sciences.

Jansi Rani (1980), *Learning Needs of the Adults*, Master Dissertation, Sri Venkateswara University.

Karve Institute of Social Sciences (1994), *Evaluation of the Literacy Campaign,* Parbhani District, Pune: KISS.

Kishore Attavar (1994), *Evaluation of Literacy Campaign,* Shimoga District, Bangalore: School of Social Work.

Krishna Murthy and Others (1992), *Evaluation of the Total Literacy Campaign,* Chittoor District, A Report, Hyderabad: The University of Hyderabad.

Madras Institute of Development Studies (1982), *Adult Education Programme in Tamil Nadu: An Appraisal of the Programme Implementation by the Universities and Colleges, Madras. MIDS.*

Madras Institute of Development Studies (1993), *Evaluation of Literacy Campaign: Kamarajar District of Tamil Nadu 1992.* Madras. MIDS.

Michale Tharakan (1990), *The Ernakulam District Total Literacy Programme, Report of Evaluation*, Trivandrum: Centre for Development Studies.

Mastaq Ahmad (1992), *An Evaluation on Total Literacy Campaign of Midnapur District (West Bengal),* New Delhi: NLM Authority.

Mustaq Ahmad (1994), *Evaluation of Literacy Campaign Almora*, Lucknow: State Resource Centre.

On Mehta and Others (1994), *Evaluation of Literacy Campaign Durg District, Cited in Evaluation of Literacy Campaign: Summary Report*, New Delhi: Govt. of India.

Paul Valiakanadathil and Savavanan (1993), *Evaluation of Literacy Campaign*, Mandya District, Bangalore: Indian Social Science Institute.

Sardar Patel Institute of Economic and Social Research (1993), *Evaluation of Literacy Campaign, Kheda District,* Ahmedabad: SPIESR.

Sardar Patel Institute of Economics and Social Research (1993), *Evaluation of Literacy Campaign Ahmedabad Rural, Ahmedabad: SPIESR.*

Sardar Patel Institute of Economics and Social Research (1993), *Evaluation of Literacy Campaign Bhav Nagar City*, Ahmedabad: SPIESR.

Sardar Patel Institute of Economics and Social Research (1994), *Evaluation of Literacy Campaign of Dang District*, Ahmedabad: SPIESR.

Sardar Patel Institute of Economic and Social Research (1994), *Evaluation of Literacy Campaign of Sundar Nagar District*, Ahmedabad: SPIESR.

Shanta Mohan (1994), *Evaluation of Literacy Campaign Dakshina Kannada*, Bangalore: Institute of Social and Economic Change.

Shastri and Chariyulu (1993), *Evaluation of Literacy Campaign West Godavari District*, Hyderabad: NIRD.

Sidda Gowda (1996), Akshara Vani, *External Report of Total Literacy Campaign, Chitradurga District, Karnataka Mysore*: Mysore University.

State Resource Centre (1996): *The Evaluation of Literacy Campaign (Andhra Pradesh)* Hyderabad, Andhra Mahila Sabha.

Tata Institute of Social Sciences (1993), Evaluation of Literacy Campaign, Nanded, Bombay: TISS.

Tata Institute of Social Sciences (1993), *Evaluation of Literacy Campaign,* Latur, Bombay: TISS.

Tata Institute of Social Sciences (1993), *Evaluation of Literacy Campaign,* Pune Rural, Bombay: TISS.

Tribal and Harijan Research Cum Training Institute (1993), *Evaluation of Literacy Campaign, Sundergarh, Bhubaneshwar:* THRTI.

Unesco (1972), *Literacy 1969-71 Progress Achieved in Literacy Through Out the World,* Paris.

Index

L

M

N